Follow
Your
Heart

African American Music
in Global Perspective

Portia K. Maultsby and Mellonee V. Burnim,
Series Editors
Archives of African American Music
and Culture Indiana University

A list of books in the series appears
at the end of this book.

Follow Your Heart

Moving with
the Giants of
Jazz, Swing, and
Rhythm and Blues

Joe Evans

with
Christopher Brooks

Forewords by Tavis Smiley
and Bill McFarlin

University of Illinois Press
Urbana and Chicago

Library of Congress Cataloging-in-Publication Data
Evans, Joe, 1916 –
Follow your heart : moving with the giants of jazz, swing, and rhythm
and blues / Joe Evans ; with Christopher Brooks.
p. cm. — (African American music in global perspective)
Includes discography (p.   ) and index.
ISBN-13 978-0-252-03303-2 (cloth : alk. paper)
ISBN-10 0-252-03303-5 (cloth : alk. paper)
1. Evans, Joe, 1916–   2. Jazz musicians—United States—Biography.
3. Rhythm and blues musicians—United States—Biography.
I. Brooks, Christopher Antonio
II. Title.
ML419.E96A3   2008
781.65092—dc22 [B]   2007030328

Contents

Foreword

Tavis Smiley

The life story of Joe Evans as voiced in *Follow Your Heart* will touch your spirit. This moving account of an unsung musician and record company executive who is now in his nineties should be required reading.

Joe Evans shared the stage with great musical icons like Billie Holiday, Bill "Bojangles" Robinson, Johnny Hodges, Nat "King" Cole, Louis Armstrong, Cab Calloway, and Charlie Parker, and *Follow Your Heart* brings these extraordinary personalities to life. Most of us have only read about these legends, heard their recordings, or seen them on television.

While people of my generation will certainly be able to relate to Ray Charles, Berry Gordy, and the Manhattans, there are stories here from which the younger generation can learn. The social commentary about the African American experience from the 1910s into the twenty-first century, which Joe Evans has lived through, gives all of us a clear view of the past and how we need to avoid repeating certain mistakes.

If there is anything such as a great generation, Joe Evans is, without a doubt, a shining example of it. What a wonderful career and life Joe Evans has had. *Follow Your Heart* is a fantastic read.

Foreword

Bill McFarlin

*F*ollow Your Heart is historically compelling and beautifully written. The book chronicles several eras of American popular music as the saxophonist and record company executive Joe Evans lived them. The importance of the story is underscored because of the dwindling number of musicians who can share their experiences of playing with historical figures such as Charlie Parker, Billie Holiday, Al Hibbler, Louis Armstrong, Jay McShann, Cab Calloway, and Andy Kirk when they were all in their prime. This book provides a unique opportunity to gain insight into the lives of these musical pioneers and to understand what motivated them and inspired their exceptional genius and talent.

For rhythm and blues enthusiasts, Evans has an equally compelling story to tell about personalities like Ivory Joe Hunter and about his own participation in the early Motown years and his foray into the music business as a founder of Carnival Records.

Evans takes us on his musical journey with humor, honesty, and integrity. He tells of the tragedies that befell many African American musicians, reminding us that although we have made significant strides for civil rights in the music industry and in our society, there is still much work to be done. Evans emerges as a living symbol of what our nation should regard with pride; his story represents not only the inequalities faced by so many great musicians but also their extraordinary achievements.

I encourage everyone to walk through history in the shoes of Joe Evans. There are many life lessons to be learned within the pages of this book.

Preface

Christopher Brooks

I t is not often that an author gets to say, "This is the story I was born to tell," but in the case of *Follow Your Heart,* it is an accurate and appropriate statement. I first met Joe Evans in fall 1994 when he audited my African American music course at Virginia Commonwealth University, and I immediately took notice of this elderly man in a sea of moderately interested undergraduates. When we began discussing "Ma" Rainey, he volunteered after class that he had actually met her. When we discussed Louis Armstrong, he said he had performed with him. This pattern continued with famous performers like Charlie Parker, Lionel Hampton, Billie Holiday, John Coltrane, and Ivory Joe Hunter, and I encouraged him to share his comments with the whole class. In subsequent meetings with Joe Evans, I came to appreciate not only the depth and breadth of his personal knowledge of jazz and popular music, but how he negotiated his way through the often challenging maze of living as an African American musician during times I had only read about.

Realizing that this was a story waiting to be shared with a wide audience, I set out to help Joe Evans write this book. Because Evans performed in so many popular American genres, this account contains names familiar to many readers. But there are other great musicians like Ray Shep and Floyd "Horsecollar" Williams whose names might be lost to history were it not for the telling of this story. At over ninety years old, Joe Evans is the repository of an incredible amount of contemporary American popular music history. Beginning in spring 1995, I typically interviewed him at his home, with his wife, Anna, sitting nearby. I also traveled to New York to speak with various individuals and held numerous telephone interviews with others around the country.

The story that emerged is an amazing one, and I am deeply honored to have played a part in its telling.

Acknowledgments

Christopher Brooks

J oe Evans and I are pleased to acknowledge those who assisted us and those who helped to prepare this book in its final form. It is because of their belief in the importance of this story that *Follow Your Heart* has come to be realized.

At the outset, I must acknowledge the role of Joe Evans's beloved wife, Anna Mae Evans (1923–99). Long before I arrived on the scene in the early 1990s, she believed this was a story that needed to be told, and when Joe Evans and I came together, she played a pivotal role in moving the project along. Were it not for her recollection of various events and individuals, the Joe Evans story would have contained noticeable gaps. This work is therefore dedicated to her memory.

I gratefully acknowledge the financial assistance I received from the Virginia Commonwealth University Grant-in-Aid Program and the Office of the Dean of the College of Humanities and Sciences. This funding was of immeasurable importance.

As this was the first time I assisted with a full-length biography, I enlisted the aid of several editors, readers, and other assistants. I am pleased to thank Dika Newlin (recently deceased), Jon Spencer, and Elizabeth Tournquist for their editorial assistance. I also thank Arlisa Polite for transcribing hours of interviews, and my graduate student at the University of Maryland, Brian Clancy, for valuable help in the early stage of this work.

I want especially to acknowledge Carole Hall, my master editor and literary consultant. Also in this category is Jay Whaley, my Richmond-based editor, advisor, and counselor, who has never failed to offer me keen insights on writing and research strategies.

Many others provided input and assistance in the writing and producing of *Follow Your Heart.* They include my brother, Carroll Brooks; Bob Daniels; Louise Fleming; Mitzi Sheppard Beck; Doris Payne; Carolyn Parker; Carrie Saunders; Esther Vassar; Brenda Kahari; and my students Katherine Blanche and Stephen Hicks. My colleagues at Virginia Commonwealth University, Audrey Smedley, Murry DePillars, Norrece Jones, Kathryn Murphy-Judy, and Patricia Cummins, shared with me their knowledge and expertise.

At the University of Illinois Press, Joan Catapano's persistence throughout the acquisition process deserves the highest praise, respect, and admiration. I want to acknowledge my copy editor, Carol Betts, who assisted me with grace and humor. I also thank those involved in the design, production, and marketing of the book for their hard work.

Before his death in 2001, Joe Evans's childhood friend Bobby Johnson spoke with me at length about his memories of their growing up in Pensacola, Florida. I also received invaluable assistance from several individuals familiar with Joe Evans's professional life, including the late, great Jay McShann, Adrian Crosdell, Al Jefferson, Toye Kates, and John Compton and Fred Robinson (aka Sir Johnny "O" and Rockin' Robin, respectively, of Baltimore radio station WWIN). I am especially pleased to thank Victor Kaply, the long-time associate of Joe Evans, who believed in this work from the beginning and shared my determination to see it in print.

I thank several people whose steady support made my task easier. Marva Williams played a significant behind-the-scenes role in the development of this work. I am also deeply indebted to Portia Maultsby, my mentor since my days as a graduate student in Texas. She has been a dear friend and supporter throughout my entire academic career. Finally, I want to thank my son, Arthur, for his constant support. He has experienced at first hand the humor, wisdom, and grace of Joe Evans, who has been like a grandfather to him. To all of you, Joe and I offer our heartfelt thanks.

follow your heart

part
one

chapter one

Pensacola Blues

One day in 1921, when I was about five, I heard a fishman on a horse-drawn wagon singing a song. Between the pauses, he blew what looked like a cow's horn, alerting people on the outskirts of Pensacola, Florida, that he was in our area selling fish. His tune went like this:

> They call me raggedy, call me raggedy, 'cause my
>   clothes are in pawn (blows horn),
> Call me raggedy, call me raggedy, 'cause my clothes are
>   in pawn (blows horn),
> But when you see me tomorrow (blows horn),
> I'll have my best clothes on (blows horn).

This was my first encounter with the twelve-bar blues. Young as I was, I felt something click deep inside me. For the first time, I had a feeling that was almost as haunting and soulful as the fishman's voice. That feeling became a touchstone for the rest of my life.

A while later I felt it again when I first heard the celebrated blues singer Bessie Smith. I was standing outside the stage door of the Belmont Theater downtown. My mother, who I called "Muh," was holding my hand. We could hear a woman singing inside. She had a low voice. It sounded as if she was moaning, like women I always heard in church.

In fact, Bessie's appearance had the feel of a church revival meeting. Inside the theater, the crowd called out to her, "Bessie! Bessie! Sing them blues!" And she gave them what they came for: "Love oh love, oh careless love . . ."

People were just screaming. A few women must have fainted, because I saw them being lifted over people's heads and carried out of the theater. Muh put her head down and began shaking her head to the music. I don't think she realized it, but she began squeezing my hand very tight. It got me caught up in the excitement, too. Hearing Bessie brought back that feeling I had when I heard the fishman's song.

Today, nearly eighty-five years later, I still love the blues. I have been all over the world and played with hundreds of great musicians, but I never got over and never forgot the impact of that rhythm, those melodies and words.

* * * * *

Although I grew up in Pensacola, most of my immediate family was from the town of Bonifay, about thirty miles east. I knew my mother's family, the Allens, pretty well. Grandpa (which is all I knew him as) and Mattie Allen had eight children: my mother, Olivia, the oldest; her sisters, Viola and Lee; and three brothers, Elijah, James, and Johnny. Later on there were two younger sisters, Jewel and Mary.

Dad's side of the family wasn't as easy to trace as Muh's. In fact, I didn't know anything about my paternal grandparents. Dad had a twin brother, Josiah Evans, and an older brother, Jasper. As far as I knew, that was it for him.

Muh married Joseph Evans Sr. around 1913, and I was born on October 7, 1916. I was nicknamed "Little" Joe since I took after my father.

Daddy worked at a local mill. Uncle Josiah was a dock foreman. He gave me nickels every time he saw me. One nickel was a treat, but he sometimes gave me three or four at a time. I was in pure heaven, because that was a lot of money. Daddy was a lean, short man with a dark complexion and round face. He was a relatively quiet man, but the front porch seemed to be his favorite place in every house we lived in. Sometimes I would sit on the steps when he was there, not saying a word. I was just content to have him nearby. Uncle Josiah sometimes stopped by and sat with us.

One of Daddy's porch rituals was to clean and polish his extensive gun collection. Once, while Uncle Josiah was admiring a particular gun, Daddy pulled the trigger. A bullet in the chamber went off, grazing Uncle Josiah. The impact knocked him off his feet. Slowly Uncle Josiah put his hand to his forehead, so I knew he wasn't dead. Daddy dropped the gun immediately and rushed to his brother.

"I didn't know there was a bullet in it!"

"You damn near killed me," Uncle Josiah said as he pulled out a handkerchief and put it to his forehead. When he pulled it away, I could see the blood. Daddy helped Uncle Josiah onto the steps of the porch and ran into the house to call someone. After he came back, Uncle Josiah said he was okay. He was speaking a little loud even though Daddy was sitting right next to him. Daddy leaned his head down on his lap and covered it with his hands and just shook from side to side. He and Uncle Josiah sat together like that for what seemed like a long time without saying a word.

I went over to the steps, sat a few steps below the men, and wrapped my arm around Daddy's leg. I lay my head on it. His leg was shaking as if he was nervous, so I held on more tightly, thinking it would help the situation.

I was about four or five when this happened, but I was nervous about guns for years. Even the sound scared me.

* * * * *

Daddy's quiet manner was not to be misunderstood for weakness. I'd seen him run off white door-to-door salesmen who acted disrespectfully to Muh. I thought that was courageous. Once, he took me on a walk and we passed a group of black men in a chain gang, with a white man standing over them with a rifle. Wearing no shirts and covered in sweat, they dug a ditch with picks and shovels. Daddy glanced at me.

"If you don't work hard in school, that's what you'll be doing when you grow up," he said. There was something very commanding in his voice. Even today, I can hear that no-nonsense tone. When he spoke that was the end of it. No one questioned him—except my mother.

Muh was short and kind of plumpish with a nice figure. She was brown skinned, with her hair pulled back in a knot. She was noticeably bowlegged but wore her clothes well. It made me proud to see her dressed up.

Most days, she cooked for at least two white families, the Coes and the

Watsons. Sometimes I went to work with her and she made breakfast for me at their houses. It was kind of exciting to pretend that I lived there.

I was the apple of Muh's eye. When she made gingerbread cookies I got to lick the bowl. When I sat on her lap she was always hugging me and petting me up. She rubbed my face and head and it made me feel good.

In the fall of 1921, however, my cherished position on her lap disappeared. One evening after Dr. McGee was at our house, I came in from playing outside. There was Muh in the bed. She looked tired, like she had been sweating, because her hair was out of place. When I got closer, I saw she was holding this little thing that looked like a doll wrapped in a white blanket with a little brown face showing. I thought Dr. McGee had brought it, and I thought to myself, "When is he coming back to get it?"

I said, "Who is this? When is he going to leave?"

"He's not going anywhere. He is going to stay here with you," Muh said. I tried to figure out where I fit into the picture now. I thought I was the only one who was supposed to be getting that kind of attention.

While she was nursing Roy Lee I would try to get up in her lap, but she made me get down. More than once I pinched Roy Lee in his crib. Once, I pinched him as hard as I could and he cried so hard that he only stopped to take breaths. Before I could run off, Muh caught me.

"What did you do to that baby?"

"Nothin'," I lied. She slapped the devil out of me.

Gradually she encouraged me to hold him, kiss and hug him. Sometimes, I'd watch him when she was outside hanging up clothes. I began to look out after Roy Lee. I remember it like yesterday when he first started to walk. I think I was more excited than Muh was to see my little baby brother moving around. He became very attached to me, and I relished my role as big brother.

• • • • •

In those days, I was kind of a loner with a Tom Sawyer kind of spirit. I set traps in the woods to catch animals. There was plenty of space where we lived on the outskirts of town and it wasn't dangerous. If I found things like old bottles, I would clean them and sell them. I went into junk yards, got the lights out of the old cars, and sold those as well.

When I was about eight, though, we moved into town. My movement seemed a little more restricted than it had been when we lived further out. Roy Lee and I could have walked to most places, but Muh always gave us orders.

"Don't cross that street!"

"Stay on this side of the street."

"Don't go on so-and-so's grass because they have a mean dog!"

"Don't go in that yard."

Once Muh took me to a restricted area, stood me there, and said, "You see that? I don't want you to go over there. You can go from right here to over there." After I got bigger, my mother would go out and leave me at home with Roy Lee. She would tell us, "Don't go outside that gate." If other children came around to play, I'd have to tell them they couldn't come into our yard. They stayed outside our gate, and we played all along the side of the fence.

One of my playmates from that period was Bobby Johnson. We quickly became friends and remained so for over seventy-five years.

His mother, Hilda, was a seamstress, and she always dressed him very neatly in tailored shirts and knickers that she had made. When Muh ordered shirts for Roy Lee and me from Hilda, Bobby delivered them. I was impressed with his relative freedom—that is, his being able to walk around town on his own without supervision. He initiated conversations with grown people in ways that I wouldn't have dared to consider. He was like a little man, much older than his years.

Hilda had a huge house and occasionally took in boarders like the musicians who came into town. Bobby told me that Joe Fazio, the trumpet player from New Orleans, had stayed at his house, as did Rubin Woods with the C. S. Belton band. There soon came a time when those names meant something to me.

* * * * *

Muh and Hilda enrolled Bobby and me at the Lillie Anna James Private School, the Lillie James School for short, on Alcaniz Street. Miss Lillie's son, Daniel "Chappie" James Jr., grew up to be this country's first black four-star general. He was among Pensacola's best and brightest stars.

For a city its size in the 1920s and 30s, Pensacola also boasted a good number of black doctors, teachers, homeowners, and other professionals. Muh hoped I would become a dentist. Several black Pensacolans had been educated at Florida A&M (or "Fam C" as it was called at the time), Bethune-Cookman College, and Edward Waters College. A fortunate few had gone out of state to historically black colleges like Alabama State, Fisk, Tuskegee, or Talladega. There was a clear emphasis on education and self-help among the black community. We were taught to have high expectations.

Miss Lillie was very strict. Believe me, you did not cross her path. When I hear of school kids fighting teachers today, I am amazed. At that time you couldn't pay a kid to talk back to a teacher, much less raise their hand to one.

I remember Miss Lillie putting a kid named R.T. in a burlap potato sack and beating the hell out of him. You could see him moving around in the sack like a bagged animal. Some of the kids held back smiles, but I was just plain scared. I wouldn't even look at him getting beat. He was a bad kid and was always getting whipped. In fact, he visited that burlap sack so many times that we nicknamed it "R.T.'s sack." I swear, that boy had to be a glutton for punishment.

Another day, Miss Lillie left the classroom with instructions that a girl in the class would write down the names of anyone who talked. One boy started speaking to me, and I told him to keep quiet. When Miss Lillie returned, the girl gave her the list.

"All of you whose names that I call, come up here," she said. I'll be damned if that girl didn't put my name and the boy's who was talking to me on the list. My heart sank with fear. That meant at least five swats on the hand with Miss Lillie's leather strap.

She was a big woman with muscular arms. I stood in line waiting for my licks. When my turn came I put out my hand. Whoop! I was scared of that woman.

• • • • •

The school always put on an annual end-of-the-year play. The one that I recall being in was *Overall Jim and Sunbonnet Sue.* I was playing the part of Overall Jim. I was so nervous, not so much because I was standing in front of an audience, but because I was afraid that I would forget some of my lines. If you forgot, that meant that you were going to get your ass beat or, worse, a visit to R.T.'s sack. I started to stutter at one point in the play as I was reciting my part. I kept repeating my line hoping that my next line would come to me, as my knees got weak. Thank God, someone helped me out by reminding me of my next line and I was able to finish my speech. I don't know who my prompter was, but I sure was thankful to him.

I was in Miss Lillie James's school about two years. During that time Bobby got beat so bad that his mother withdrew him from the school. When Muh sent me to public school, P.S. 44, I must have been around twelve. Roy Lee was there already, but several grades behind me. Muh told us that we should be careful not to mess up our school clothes, and there was to be no fighting. By this time, I had learned never to cross a strict woman.

* * * * *

One day, when Roy Lee and I were on our way home, some boys from another school tried to start a fight. I ran off so fast I lost one of my brand new shoes. It wasn't until I got close to home that I realized that Roy Lee wasn't with me. He had stayed behind.

When Muh saw me she said, "Where is your brother?"

"He's down the street, fighting."

"Fighting?"

"Yeah, some boys jumped us and I ran."

"You ran!?"

"Yes, ma'am."

"You get back down there and find your brother! And where is your shoe?"

"I don't know. I must have run out of it."

"Boy, you get back down there and get your brother."

I went back for Roy Lee and found him on his way home.

"What did you do?" I asked him.

"They wanted to fight, so I gave them a fight," he replied. He said that he hit one of the boys in the eye and the others let him alone.

When we got home, Muh said, "What were you doing out there fighting?"

Roy Lee said, "Some boys stopped us and wanted to fight, and Joe ran off."

"I'm going to get him for running off," she said.

I was confused. She had told us not to fight, but I was getting punished for following her instructions. She told me that I shouldn't have run off and left my brother. I also got a whipping for losing one of my shoes, which I never found.

So I decided I had to start fighting. Sometimes, I wouldn't even wait for someone to throw the first punch. They'd call me a name and I'd say, "What'd you say?" and start fighting. Once these two German brothers called me "leettle neeggah Joe," in their thick German accents, and I started fighting both of them. One of them got me around the neck, but I had ahold of the other one and wouldn't let him go. I also had a railroad spike in my hand. I told the one who had me around the neck, "If you hit me again, I'm going to hit your brother with this spike." The boy hit me in the back of my head with something and I made good on my threat to his brother. Blood spurted everywhere. I got scared and stopped.

The brothers went home hollering. It wasn't too long before their mother came to my house with the one that I had hit.

"Look what your boy did to my boy," she said to Muh. He was still bleeding.

"Look at *my* boy," Muh said. She turned me around to show the woman that I also had a cut on the head that I'd gotten when I was hit by her other son. Then Muh suggested, "Since we both have to go to the doctor, I guess I just have to pay for my boy and you have to pay for yours. And you need to straighten them out about fighting, because they jumped on him and that's why he was fighting them."

Later, Muh took me inside and said, "Look here, I told you that you have to fight sometimes, but I didn't mean for you to go and pick fights. You have to try to avoid them if possible. If someone attacks you, then you can fight. Outside of that, you need to tell people that you don't want to fight."

As always, I tried to do what she said, but I became especially protective of Roy Lee. Even though we would fight with each other, I wouldn't let anyone else hit him. I didn't even like it when Muh hit him. When she wanted to beat him for something, she would send me outside to get a switch. I would bring back the smallest one that I could find and would tell her that that's the best that I could do. When the situation was reversed, however, Roy Lee would come back in the house with a broom handle or something even thicker and I would start crying in advance of the whipping. She'd tell him, "I can't beat this boy with that!" But I couldn't stand it when Roy Lee was being punished. It was like I was feeling it. So when Muh was beating him, I would jump in the way to take some of his licks or distract her in some way by telling her that someone was at the door.

I remember the time that we both got our tonsils out at Pensacola Hospital. I believe it was operated by the Catholic Church because there were so many nuns around. They took Roy Lee into the operating room first and I was on a stretcher waiting to go in after him. When they rolled him out past me, he wasn't moving and his mouth was wide open.

"You killed my brother!" I jumped up and yelled. I was ready to fight. It took several of the nuns to control me. They put me back on the stretcher, strapped me down to the gurney, and gave me the ether. The next thing that I remember was waking up in the room with Roy Lee in the bed next to me.

· · · · ·

When I was around twelve, Roy Lee and I were baptized together in an outlet of the Pensacola Bay. We waded out in the water in our white nightshirts. Reverend Deampert was standing there. He dipped us backwards under the water while holding our heads. At the Sixth Avenue Baptist Church on the east side of town, Sunday was an all-day and evening affair. In the morning it was Sunday school, followed by 11 A.M. service. In the afternoon there was the Baptist Young People's Union (commonly known as BYPU) followed by a night service that started around 7:30 P.M. and went for a couple of hours.

Roy Lee was bored in church more easily than I was. Once we were singing an up-tempo version of "Give Me That Old Time Religion," and this ample woman sitting between Roy Lee and me who routinely "got happy" every Sunday jumped up with her arms swinging while the singing was picking up speed. Some of the ushers came over to fan her and keep her from hurting herself. After a few minutes, they managed to sit her down, but Roy Lee had placed a tack where her hips hit the seat. She jumped with a scream, "Oh, Lord!" leading the ushers to believe she was getting happy again.

I remember telling Muh when I was about sixteen that there were two things that I wasn't going to do when I was grown. First, I wasn't taking any more castor oil, which was a Saturday morning ritual for Roy Lee and me. She asked me what was the second thing. I told her that I wasn't going to church. She had a fit, but I was determined. I kept the first resolution for sure, but I didn't keep the second one.

chapter two

Music Crazy

Once the music bug bit me, it became my obsession and my passion. It was as if the rest of my childhood quickly sped away. Music eventually became my great discovery, but the initial path was a bumpy one.

Muh really wanted me to play an instrument. She also decided that the violin was what she wanted me to play. I can't say that I felt one way or the other about it at first, but I took about four or five lessons. One afternoon, I was coming home from a lesson and some boys started to tease me about playing the violin. What made matters worse was that I was also wearing knickers, for which young boys were often ridiculed by their peers.

"Man, you're going to be a little sissy. Look at you," one boy called out.

"What's that you called me?"

"You heard me!"

I started hitting the boy with my violin case. At some point, the case came open. The violin fell out, and I stepped on it. I picked it up and hit the boy across the head with it. When I looked down in my hand, all I had was the neck of the instrument, with the strings hanging down holding the body.

"Look what you made me do," I said. I was ready to go crazy on the boy by then, but he ran off. I started crying because I knew what Muh's reaction was going to be when she saw that violin.

As soon as I reached the front door and saw Muh, I cried, "Look what those boys made me do!?"

"The *boys* made you do!? Boy, you broke that violin!"

"They called me a sissy."

"That doesn't matter, words don't hurt you! You had no business breaking that violin!"

Sensing that my blaming strategy wasn't going to work, I thought quickly, "And furthermore, I don't like nobody to talk about my mother."

"Talking about your mother? What'd they say?"

"They were playing the dozens with me, and I couldn't stand it no more and that's why I broke the violin over the boy's head." I was lying, of course, but it seemed to have saved me because she was all set to give me a proper whipping.

"Well, all right, you get in there and clean up, but that's the end of your musician day," she said.

But Muh was still determined. One day when I got home there was a brand new piano in the front living room. I thought it was pretty, but aside from that it really didn't impress me. She said that if I took piano lessons, I didn't have to carry the instrument and that I would be able to play at other people's houses and for my own enjoyment.

That's how I started taking lessons with Professor Bennett. A short, dark man with glasses, he looked as if he could have been an African. He carried a long pencil during the lessons, and if you made a mistake he would pop you on the fingers. Once, when I was en route to a lesson, some boys invited me to play baseball. I told them no, but they said I could play just a couple of innings. I took off my coat and before I realized it, I had missed the lesson, so I turned around and went back home. When I got there I did a few scales up and down the keyboard to make my mother believe that I had been to my lesson. I skipped a couple more lessons to play baseball, but Muh was still sending the money to Professor Bennett. Eventually, he came to our house and told her that I had stopped coming. Well, she whipped my ass and that was the end of my second attempt at musicianhood.

The third time must have been the charm. I believe it was because, unlike the other times, the desire to play was coming from within me.

As I was riding my bicycle one afternoon, I saw a band playing on a truck to advertise an upcoming performance. The band turned out to be the Midnight Owls, who were led by Raymond Sheppard, a well-known local musician usually known as Ray Shep. They were playing "Tiger Rag." The trombonist, whose name I later learned was also Evans, took off his shoe and used his foot to produce several slides on his instrument. I reasoned that the trombone couldn't be that hard to play because all you had to do was blow and move that slide back and forth. It was fantastic. I also noticed a boy on the truck playing saxophone. He had to be around thirteen or fourteen, my age, which was even more astounding!

I went home and told Muh that the trombone was the instrument that I wanted to play. I thought that she would be happy about my long-awaited announcement. I was finally ready to play an instrument, but she just shrugged and said I wasn't serious. Predictably, she recounted my past attempts at being a musician, as evidenced by the unplayed piano in the living room and the broken violin. But I told her that the boys had teased me for playing the piano and the violin. Still, she said she was not paying for any more lessons. If I wanted to play, I had to pay for my own lessons. I was so determined that I used the money that I had accumulated in a savings account from my various jobs.

What made me realize I was serious about playing the trombone was that I even found my own teacher. I saw kids going to and from this house with their instrument cases, and I asked one of them who their teacher was. It turned out to be a Professor Seymour, who taught several instruments, including trombone. He was maybe in his early forties, because he had some strands of gray hair in his head. He wore glasses, and a dark brown beret topped his tall frame. Like Professor Bennett, my former piano teacher, I never knew his first name.

I went to see him to schedule my first lesson. He lived and taught in a residential home in which he rented a room and a studio on West Belmont Street. When we met, I told him I wanted to play the trombone. He told me he didn't have a trombone available at the time because some other student had rented it.

"What about the saxophone?" he said.

"No, if you don't have a trombone, I'll play the trumpet because it only has three keys." He wasn't taking no for an answer, though.

"Listen, the saxophone has all these keys. All you do is press the key for the note. With the trumpet, you've got to make all the same notes that the guys make with the saxophone, but you only got three keys to do it with. Come on and try it."

"I don't know, I want to be . . ."

"Come on. Try it," he said.

He took a bright, shining saxophone off his wall of instruments as if to tempt me with it. He showed me where to place my fingers on the keys and how to blow through the mouthpiece. I lifted my fingers off of the keys as he instructed me and out came the notes, C-D-E-F-G-A-B-C, the C scale. When I finished, he said with enthusiasm, "You see what you just did!? It would have taken you three months to do that on the trumpet or trombone. Those instruments with fewer or no keys require you to develop your lip." He actually used the word "embouchure" but it didn't mean anything to me at the time. His psych job worked. I was convinced. I told him with all of the certainty in the world that I would play the saxophone.

He gave me a chart to learn the notes and said, "You come back and see me when you learn those notes and I'll start you on your lessons." I was back the very next day, because I had memorized the chart overnight. I remember the look of surprise on his round, dark face. He wasn't expecting me.

"You know all the notes that I gave you?"

"Yes, sir!"

"Give me that sheet that I gave you." I handed it to him and he began to quiz me right on the spot and began pointing to various notes on the sheet.

"What is that note?"

"C."

"What about that?"

"F."

He asked me another and I told him.

"What'd you do? Stay up all night?"

"No, sir, I just kept looking at them." I could see in his eyes and posture that he was impressed with what I had done.

"You really want to play, don't you, son?" he said. I nodded without saying anything, and we began our lessons right then and there.

I paid fifty cents per lesson. I told him that I didn't have my own saxophone. He asked me if my parents would buy me one, but I told him about my mother's firm position not to buy me another instrument. He had a saxophone that I could use for the lesson, but I couldn't take it home for practicing. He had the music already and assigned me scales and simple songs, which I mastered very easily. At home, I used a broomstick to practice my fingerings just like it was a saxophone. Professor Seymour taught me all of the fingerings, the scales, and the note values. He also taught me about the importance of breath control and embouchure. It took about one month for me to master all of the fundamentals.

Professor Seymour played bass tuba with a local band called Rubin Johnson and the Florida Ramblers. One day, after I had been studying with him for about two or three months, he was returning from a playing date when the car hit a bump or a ditch. Professor Seymour's head hit the top of the car so hard, he received a neck injury that must have also injured his spine. He was paralyzed from the neck down. The first time that I tried to see him after the accident, the landlady said he couldn't have any visitors. I kept thinking his injury wasn't as bad as I had heard and after a brief rest he and I could get back to work.

When I did get in to see him, he was bedridden. A large brace circled his neck. I had to get up close to the bed to hear him speak. It was barely a whisper. He appeared to be in pain as he tried to talk.

"Son, are you still practicing?"

"Yes, sir, Professor Seymour," I said.

"Well, you keep working hard." The moment was so awkward for me I could only manage to ask him how he felt, and he said not well.

"Professor Seymour, sir, is there anything you want me to do for you?" He whispered, "No." I stayed a few minutes longer and left.

I wanted to go to see him every day, but Muh thought I would be talking to him about music and she wanted me to leave him alone so he could rest. When I did go back a second time, the lady at the boardinghouse told me he had died. I was saddened because I had come to see him as my link to musical understanding and enjoyment. If there had been a funeral I would have gone, but I understood that some of his relatives came to town to claim his remains and shut down his studio. I didn't get a chance to say good-bye.

For a moment, I thought that God was teaching me a lesson about being serious and not taking things for granted. When I had the opportunity to study and play, I wasn't serious. Now that I really wanted to play, I lost my teacher.

I still practiced my fingerings on that broomstick faithfully and did not lose my enthusiasm about playing the saxophone. Bobby Johnson, my best friend, stopped by one day with a new trumpet from his father in Cleveland. He took it out and started blowing a melody that resembled "I'm Confessing," which was later made popular by Louis Armstrong. I was amazed. Professor Seymour had told me it would take a long time to play basic notes on the trumpet.

"How'd you do that? Who taught you that?"

"Nobody. It was easy," he said.

I soon learned his secret. Bobby had perhaps the best and, without a doubt, the most authoritarian trumpet teacher in town, Mr. Joe Jessie. Mr. Joe Jessie was a severe man who would whack your hands good and hard if you made a mistake. You were expected to say, "yes, sir," and "no, sir." He often spoke about a New Orleans trumpeter whom he admired named Buddy Petite.

Years later when I was with the Ray Shep band, of which Mr. Joe Jessie was also a member, he was every bit as authoritarian as he had ever been. He eventually met with a tragic death at the hands of one his trumpet students. In 1936, he had disciplined this boy during a lesson (which included several raps on the boy's hands). The boy, who was mildly retarded, returned to the house with a gun and shot Mr. Joe Jessie dead.

· · · · ·

Muh felt sorry for me for having just lost my teacher. Seeing Bobby's enthusiasm with his new trumpet, and me still practicing my saxophone fingerings on that broomstick, she decided that I was now serious about studying music. One day I came home from school and saw what appeared to be a saxophone case on the dining room table. I didn't dare touch it or even get close to it. I rushed to Muh in the kitchen.

"What's in that case in the dining room?"

She asked half-seriously, "What case?"

"That case on the dining room table."

"What does it look like?"

"It looks like an instrument."

"You can open it."

I did, and there was a brand-new shiny saxophone! I thought my eyes would pop out of my head. I was so excited that my heart was racing. Just to play it safe, I asked, "Whose saxophone is this?"

"I'll give you three guesses."

I took it out of the case and put it together and attached the supporting strap. At that moment it was as if time stood still. I started playing scales and some of the passages that I had learned with Professor Seymour, and it was at least an hour before Muh told me I had to put the instrument away and do my schoolwork.

I was so committed to playing that I practiced at all hours, day and night. I wore that saxophone out. I'd play in the morning before I went to school, and when I got home I would continue in the evening. Eventually, neighbors came over to our house to complain that I was keeping them up at night. Muh restricted my practicing to two hours in the afternoon after I got back from school. But I would sometimes sneak out to the shed in the backyard, close the door, and play softly.

Within seven months, I was playing first alto saxophone in the Washington High School orchestra. To practice, I asked one or two of the kids to join me to play through our parts and then switch parts. We sometimes went to the music store and bought sheet music and played through it. Some of us also played outside jobs together. Bobby played trumpet, and the second tenor saxophonist, Robert Willis, who we called "Snookie," turned out to be the same boy that I had seen playing on the truck. One day Snookie and I competed against each other in an after-school recital. I played the Neapolitan song "O Sole Mio" and received a sizable applause from the students in the auditorium. I felt confident of my success, until Snookie played a saxophone arrangement of Franz Schubert's "Serenade." Then, he improvised on that melody and, I must say, played the hell out of it. Needless to say, he won the competition.

I realized that I still needed a teacher. I started asking around who taught saxophone. I even tried to find out who Robert Willis studied with, but I was too proud to ask him directly. Someone told me that he studied with Raymond Sheppard. I had heard his group, the Midnight Owls, play on the radio and even seen him playing on that truck. It turned out that he lived just two blocks away from me, so I went over and introduced myself right away. My initial meeting with Raymond Sheppard marked a dramatic change in my life. I told him that I had studied saxophone briefly with Professor Seymour. He nodded his acknowledgment that I had studied with a good person. He questioned me on how serious I was about playing the instrument. I bought an instruction book that he had written. We didn't schedule a lesson that day, but over the years he taught me how to play, arrange, and transpose music, and a whole lot more. I learned lessons from him that have lasted me a lifetime.

* * * * *

I had just started working with Shep when things changed on the home front. Daddy had taken a job in Bessemer, Alabama. I believe he was a foreman at a steel mill. It was a much better paying job, to be sure. He wanted to move the whole family to Bessemer. Muh wasn't keen on the idea, because Alabama had a much worse reputation as far as race relations were concerned than where we lived in Florida. Even then, we were hearing horror stories of racial attacks in Alabama and Mississippi. People said, "Hell itself wasn't as bad as Mississippi."

In the 1920s and 30s, Pensacola was relatively progressive, especially when compared to towns in Alabama and Mississippi. There was segregation in restaurants and hotels, but many institutions were integrated. Whites and blacks lived in the same neighborhood in the 1920s, but that became an increasing rarity as time went on. I had only heard about one lynching in Pensacola, which must have been in the 1920s if not earlier.

Southwest of downtown was the "tan yard" where mostly light-skinned people lived. Many of them were of Creole ancestry. Quite a few white people also lived in the tan yard. It was clear to me that some "race mixing" was going on, because sometimes I couldn't tell if someone was black or white. At that time, one-sixteenth of black blood made you black or "Negro," as we were known then.

Pensacola had developed under three different flags—French, English, and Spanish. The Spanish influence was particularly strong in the names of certain streets downtown: Alcaniz, Barcelona, DeSoto, DeVilla, Gonzalez, Tarragona, and Zaragossa.

The Pensacola Naval Air Station, I believe, had made the city more cosmopolitan than most. People from all over the country were there, not to mention the presence of a substantial immigrant community.

If Daddy had asked the family to move to Chicago or Washington, D.C., that would have been another matter. But Bessemer, Alabama, was not my idea of a swinging town with opportunities for musicians.

Daddy came home twice a month to visit, but his absence didn't affect me because I was so wrapped up in my music. I remember him lecturing me about schoolwork. He reminded me that studying music didn't make me grown. His favorite expression was, "Don't make me do . . . , boy." Trust me, neither Roy Lee or I tested him. After Dad left for Alabama, Uncle Josiah took a more prominent role in family affairs. If there was something Muh couldn't handle, she called him in. As long as I didn't have to leave my teacher, that was okay with me.

chapter three

Boy Meets Band

My first and lasting impression of Raymond Sheppard was that he was very neat. He was brown-skinned with dimples, clean shaven, and always well dressed. Even when he was giving lessons, I can't recall seeing him without a shirt and tie.

He was the younger of two brothers. Shep lived with his parents, Edward and Lilly Sheppard, at 612 North Reus Street. Lilly Sheppard was a very talkative woman who asked a lot of questions and sometimes talked even when no one was listening. She was always going on about what she would do after her husband's death, particularly her plans for his insurance policy. "When Eddy dies, Raymond and I are going to travel around the world," she would begin. The elder Mr. Sheppard, usually sitting on the porch reading a book or a paper nearby, would not even raise an eyelash. When she said things like that, Shep would stick his head out of the door and say, "Oh, Mama, hush." Shep was her pride and joy, especially after he became a successful musician.

Shep played clarinet and sang, but he was best known as an alto saxophonist, an arranger, and bandleader. His first group, the Midnight Owls,
became Ray Shep and the Midnight Owls, and eventually Ray Shep and
His Orchestra.

Even before I began to study with Shep, I had heard the band play over the
airwaves. The local radio station WCAU that broadcast from the San Carlos
Hotel at Palafox and Garden Street would feature the Midnight Owls playing
"Sweet Sue," "Vine Street Rag," "Sweet Georgia Brown," and "Eleven-Thirty
Saturday Night."

Robert "Snookie" Willis, a tenor saxophonist and a student of Shep's,
played with the band. He was the youngest member of the group at the
time. I thought how nice it must have been to be that young and able to
play and associate with all of those grown musicians. During those days you
seldom saw young people our age playing with professional musicians.

Shep was eleven years older than me. For a few years he had attended
Fisk University in Nashville, then dropped out, not because of academic
reasons, but for financial ones. He had been a classmate of the bandleader
Jimmie Lunceford at Fisk. He always talked about Lunceford's strict disci-
pline and how much he liked his style of band directing.

Growing up in Pensacola, I had the opportunity to see and hear many
of the great black territory bands, meaning those that were either based in
the region or toured from other parts of the country. I saw "Smiling" Billy
Stewart and the Celery City Serenaders from Sanford, Florida; C. S. Belton
and His Florida Society Syncopators; and the Sunset Royal Entertainers
from West Palm Beach with its members E. V. Perry and Bobby Smith. I
even worked with E. V. Perry at the Apollo Theater many years later.

From Miami came Hartley Toots and "Little" George Kelly. Although
I never heard Hartley Toots in person, I remember seeing the band pass
through South Florida when I was there with Ray Shep's band. George
Kelly had a fantastic drummer named Panama Francis, whom I also worked
with later when I was in New York. Also memorable was Don Albert from
Texas. He was so light-skinned he could pass for white, but he had a very
good band. So did Oscar "Papa" Celestin, Joe Robichaux, and Walter "Fats"
Pichon, all of whom were from New Orleans, but I saw them in Pensacola.
I also remember a group called the Carolina Cotton Pickers playing in
the area.

I especially recall seeing Walter Barnes from Chicago. He was a suave
guy, and his band was one of the best dressed groups of that period. He was
very flashy with the clarinet, but he really didn't play that well. He had ar-

rangements whereby he would play two or three notes on the instrument while good musicians in the band filled in the rest. He ended the piece holding a high note, pointing his clarinet up in the air. People would say, "That Walter Barnes is great." I heard about him having died in a fire in Mississippi, during an engagement. As I recall, only one of his musicians survived. The hall was a fire trap with only one way out. There were many places that I played in when I was touring that were not much better.

Pensacola fielded its territory bands, too. We had Rubin Johnson and the Florida Ramblers, and of course my teacher, Ray Shep.

My lessons with Shep were very structured. After I got home from school and did whatever chores Muh assigned, I went to my lesson. Shep charged more than Professor Seymour. I paid $1.50 an hour, but I was so dedicated that I sometimes showed up at Shep's house unannounced to take an extra lesson.

Shep started out teaching me from a method book, probably a Carl Fischer instruction manual. One week I would focus on breathing or holding long tones. Another week there would be an exercise on articulation using the tongue for staccato passages. Shep frequently wrote these exercises himself in the style of contemporary popular tunes, like "Mule Face Blues" or "Up a Lazy River." A particular treat for me was when he wrote short works for two saxophones and played the lead part. I would play the second part. Then we would reverse parts, with me playing the lead and him playing the second. The technical difficulties of these exercises were designed to strengthen my sight-reading skills and they did just that. Many of these pieces had a variety of arpeggios, sforzandos, staccatos, key changes, slurs, sixteenth and thirty-second notes, and the like. All of these things would sometimes be found in a single exercise. I must give credit for my strong sight-reading ability to Shep and those complex exercises that he wrote for my lessons.

When Shep realized my level of commitment, he just let me come in when he was not teaching other students and would give me unscheduled lessons. In exchange I did odd jobs around the Sheppard household, like mow the lawn, rake leaves, or sweep and mop the kitchen. I got additional practice playing with the Washington High School band, but I drilled using the exercises that Shep gave me every day.

* * * * *

About a year later, the alto saxophonist Charlie Bruton left the Midnight Owls to take a job out of town. During our next lesson, Shep asked me if I thought I could handle the job. I was about fourteen or fifteen and

I was both nervous and excited at the offer, but I managed to say I could do it. I told him, though, that I had to ask my mother.

I knew Muh would not be too receptive to the idea of my playing with a professional band. She said she knew of musicians who had contracted tuberculosis, called "consumption" at the time, and she believed it had something to do with blowing on a horn too long. To be sure, Muh talked to Dr. Sunday, one of several black physicians in town, about musicians' susceptibility to tuberculosis. I was with her in his office when he explained that it wasn't the playing that caused the musicians to contract the illness, but how they neglected to take care of themselves afterwards. For example, heavy perspiration, exposure after playing, drinking whiskey, and long hours without proper rest were contributing factors to getting colds and other illnesses. He said, in fact, that my playing the saxophone would help me to develop strong lungs.

Muh also had a specific requirement that someone from the band come and talk to her about chaperoning me. Mr. Leroy Robinson, the pianist, was appointed to talk to her. I didn't hear the conversation between him and Muh. In those days when adults spoke, children generally didn't stay around. But after Mr. Leroy left, Muh called me into the living room and told me that I had to obey him at all times, as if the directions were coming from her. If he told me to do something, I should do it. She made it clear to me that if Mr. Leroy ever came back to tell her that I disobeyed him, it would be my last night playing with them. Her other stipulations were that I could only play on the weekend and I could only travel with the group when school was out.

When I joined the band, the brass section included trumpeters Mr. Joe Jessie and Howard Hollis and trombonist Roscoe Johnson. The reeds were made up of Shep and me playing alto saxophone and Robert "Snookie" Willis playing tenor saxophone. The rhythm section was Leroy Robinson playing piano, Arthur Sawyer on drums, and Vernon Barnett on banjo and guitar. There were other members at various times, including pianist Helen Barnett (Vernon Barnett's wife); bassists D. J. Kelly and Levi Mann; pianists William Mann and Edwin Moss; tenor saxophonist Milan Bates; trumpeter Johnny Warren; and singer Cecil Williams.

Our first job was at a lodge called Williams Hall in Pensacola. We all wore Eton jackets. I was just thrown in the band, so to speak, with no rehearsal. I was nervous facing all of the people in the audience. The comforting thing was that I had Shep playing next to me, and I was already accustomed to playing with him from our lessons. At the end of the evening, I think I was more excited about being out late at night than anything else. It really made me feel grown up. When it was time to leave, I was dragging behind. Mr. Leroy yelled, "Come on, boy, come on!"

When we drove up to my house, Muh was peeping through the window to make sure it was me arriving safely. Before I could ring the doorbell, she opened the door. When Mr. Leroy saw that I was in, he nodded to her and pulled off in his car. Muh asked me how things had gone with my first professional engagement. Instead of answering her, I reached in my pocket and pulled out the thirty-five dollars I had received and put it on the table.

"What is that?"

"That's the money I made for playing," I said, feeling a little confused as to why she was acting so serious.

"You mean they gave you money for making all that noise you make around here? Don't lie to me. You tell me the truth. Where did you get that money?"

I said, "That's what they give me. Each of us got a share."

"Boy, I'm gonna give you one more chance. Where did that money come from?" Her tone was even sterner.

"That's what they give me."

"All right," Muh said. She went to the telephone and called Mr. Leroy. "Hey, Leroy. This boy came in here with a handful of money. Where did he get it?"

I heard Mr. Leroy ask, "Is it about thirty-five dollars?" Muh said it was. "That's what they paid him for playing."

Muh came back from the telephone smiling and shaking her head in disbelief. "They gave you all that money for making that noise."

* * * * *

I played with the group in a theater for the first time two weeks later. Pensacola had three theaters at the time: the Belmont, the Isis, and the Saenger. The most upscale was the Belmont Theater located on Belmont near Railroad Street. It was part of the Theater Owners Booking Association (TOBA) circuit, which meant that some of the best black talent around in those days came through its doors. You entered through a storefront with walk-up stairs. You purchased tickets at a box office. Beyond a small lobby, double doors led into the main auditorium. It seated about six hundred downstairs, but there was also a small balcony.

The Belmont catered mostly to blacks who enjoyed home-grown groups such as Butterbeans and Susie, a minstrel-like husband-and-wife comedy team. Years later when I played with them in the stage band at the Apollo

Theater, they told me that although they were based in Chicago, they were originally from Pensacola. So was "Slim" Gaillard, an outstanding guitar player and singer. Part of the duo Slim and Slam, Slim was best-known for his song "Flat Foot Floogie with the Floy Floy." He had his own stylized language, like, "I feel so bouty. Is everything booty? Is the booty bouty?" I never understood what those phrases meant, but he used them in his songs.

Shep's band was playing at the Saenger Theater on South Palafox Street. It was bigger than the Belmont. I had a small solo in one of the numbers and can't for the life of me remember what the song was, but I recall looking into the audience before I stood up to play. It seemed there were more people in that audience than I had ever seen in my entire life. There were even people up in the balcony. Bright lights were shining. As far as I could determine, the entire audience was sitting forward in their seats looking at me. Suddenly, I got weak in the knees, and my heart started pounding hard. I got short of breath, and my mouth got dry. After the number was over, I asked Shep if anything was wrong with me.

"It was only stage fright. You'll get over it," he said in a very matter-of-fact tone. His prediction was correct. I can't recall ever having stage fright again.

· · · · ·

As the youngest member of the band, I discovered how to be a grown man. Shortly after I joined the group, we added another trumpet player, my best friend, Bobby Johnson, which made us the two youngest members. Snookie Willis was a year older than we were. I bugged out at white men's private parties or what were called "smokers." In noisy smoke-filled rooms, women stripped and kissed the men and danced in front of them with their titties shaking. Some had decorated pasties on their nipples. The men, in turn, were yelling and throwing money, trying to grab them or put their hands up the women's panties. Some of the women just had V-shaped G-strings on. I confess that I was looking at the activities when I was supposed to be playing, and Shep had to nudge me on the arm more than once because I had lost my spot in the music.

One weekend the band played at a small club in Belle Glade, Florida, down near Lake Okeechobee, an area nicknamed the "Muck" because of the black dirt and good farmland. The club was a real hole-in-the-wall. Most of the people sported cuts or stab wounds or scars on their necks, arms, legs, and faces. There was one nice-looking woman at the club, but she too had a long cut on her neck. It soon became apparent how all of these wounds happened. About an hour into our playing, a fight broke out in the middle of the dance floor. Two men circled each other with switch-blades drawn. The two fighters grabbed each other by their left hands, swinging their blades with their right hands. It almost looked staged, sling-ing their blades and cutting each other. Then one of the guys fell and the other one jumped on him, stabbing him until he didn't move. The guy who won got up and stumbled out, bleeding. The other people on the floor made a path for him as he moved toward the door.

The band had played throughout the entire fight episode. After the fight was over, people continued to dance, with the dead man still on the floor. Finally, someone moved him off to the side. At our intermission I asked a man when the police were going to come.

"Are you kidding?" he said. "The police not comin' down here to fool with these niggas tonight. They don't mind as long as they killing each other. Cops'll be out here in the morning." He opened my eyes to some grim realities. While we played through that fight at the Muck, there were places where the band stopped because it had become so rowdy. When people started throwing things at the bandstand, Shep's familiar refrain was, "Behind the piano," which meant I should grab my instrument and move behind the upright piano until things settled down. He was always in front of me getting there.

●　●　●　●　●

I was with Shep's band for nearly two years when the greatest tragedy of my short life occurred. Muh had asked me to go downtown earlier that day to pay a bill. When I got back, she was in her room lying down, and that was uncommon behavior for her. When I got back she told me she didn't feel well. I was in the kitchen getting her some water when I heard a thud. She had fallen on the floor by her bed. I helped her back to the bed, but she was perspiring heavily and gasping for breath. I was so nervous. I wasn't sure what to do next, and Daddy had just left to return to Alabama. Roy Lee was playing in the backyard, so I told him to run and get the doc-tor. Dr. Sunday was away, so his office called someone else, Dr. Moon, to come to our house.

By the time Dr. Moon arrived, Muh was unconscious. Dr. Moon stayed with her for a while. Then he called me back to the room to tell me that he had done all that he could do, but that she had "expired." My first reac-tion was to cry, but I knew I had an even worse task ahead, to tell Roy Lee. I remember that he kept asking, "What's wrong? What's wrong?" When I told him that Muh had died, he wanted to go in the room to see for himself, but Dr. Moon had already pulled the sheet over her face.

As the man of the house, I tried to think how the grown men in the band would have handled themselves in this situation. When Daddy arrived he made arrangements for Morris Funeral Home to handle the funeral.

Muh's funeral was held at Sixth Avenue Baptist Church. People came to pay their respects from all over Pensacola. Shep, Mr. Leroy, Vernon Barnett, and even mean Mr. Joe Jessie came to the wake and the funeral. We buried Muh at a cemetery on North Deville Street near the Knights of Pythias Hall.

* * * * *

Daddy wanted Roy Lee and me to return with him to Alabama, but I wanted to stay in Pensacola. Besides, he wasn't getting me away from Shep's band. Being in that band made me feel like my own man. I would have run off from Daddy to get back to Shep. The family discussed it and decided that I would stay in our house temporarily to oversee the removal of the furniture and the sale of the house. Roy Lee moved in right away with Muh's sister, Aunt Lee.

After a while, I joined him there. I had my own room on an enclosed porch with a separate entrance to the house. It made me feel more independent, but I did miss the structure of home and Muh's rules.

I began playing regularly with Ray Shep. Without the supervision of Muh, I sporadically attended school. Sometimes, after being up late at night for an engagement, I was too tired or lazy to go to school the next morning. Muh never would have heard of such behavior from me. Sometimes I was so unprepared for class that the teachers kicked me out of the room.

And yet, I still played in the Washington High School band. One day, a rich white man, Mr. Gilmore, came to the school to recruit some of us to play at the clubs he owned in a suburb called Golden. Usually, Old Man Gilmore picked us up at school and took us home late at night after we played.

One night, he sent his young nephew to carry us home at about 1:00 A.M. I was sitting up front in the car, with Bobby Johnson and two other boys in the back. Our car was stopped at a light when another car sped in front of us and almost hit us. Gilmore's nephew yelled at the other driver, who continued going fast, so Gilmore's nephew took off after him.

Before long, we heard a police siren behind us and pulled to the side of the road.

"Sir, you went through that intersection back there pretty fast," the cop said very politely. The nephew was equally polite in responding, "Yes, sir. I am sorry about that. I was just taking these boys home and . . ." At that point, the cop flashed the light in the car and his polite tone turned stern. He said, "You got a bunch of niggers in here."

The nephew said again politely, "Sir, I am just trying to get these boys home . . ."

"No," the cop interrupted, "you got that wrong. Where you are going is to jail." He looked at the nephew's license and recognized the surname.

"Are you Old Man Gilmore's boy?"

"Yes, sir."

"He thinks he owns Golden out there. Follow me," the cop said in a more aggressive tone.

When we arrived at the police station, I stayed in the car. I didn't think any of us had done anything. The cop yelled, "Get out that car, nigger!"

"Me?"

"Yeah, you. Get your ass out here."

I woke Bobby up. He had slept through the whole episode. In a daze, he asked, "What happened? Where are we at?" I told him to get out and that we were at the jail house. As we were going in I whispered, "Hey, man, I don't want to go to jail, I think I'm gonna run for it."

"Run where?" Bobby said. "They'll shoot your ass before you make it any place." We went in.

"Can I call my mother?" Bobby asked. The cop snapped back, "You ain't calling no damn body. They'll find you." Eventually, Old Man Gilmore did. He was very calm when speaking to the police officers, but his nephew was mad as hell.

Later that morning, we all stood before the judge. The cop who arrested us lied. "Your honor, not only were they speeding, but those boys (pointing to us) were hollerin' and disturbing the peace." I immediately said, "No, sir, your honor. Everyone except me and the driver was sleep and I wasn't keeping up any . . ." The judge stopped me and told me to wait. I would get my chance. Without hearing me, though, the judge fined the nephew twenty-five dollars for speeding and told us to go straight to school. Mr. Gilmore took us right to the school door.

The news of our court appearance got around Washington High pretty quickly. Some of the kids began joking us, "What kind of bird doesn't fly? A jail bird." We heard it a little while before it died out.

· · · · ·

Besides music, I had only one interest at Washington High, a girl named Taudry B. Aaron. She was from a strict family that lived on the other side of town. Taudry's father was rough and not easy to deal with. Mr. Aaron walked with a limp and was known to deal harshly with anyone who acted inappropriately with his daughters. He worked just a block away from their house. At first, we did things like go to church and to an occasional movie, or to the ice cream parlor. If she managed to sneak off, we'd meet at the nearby swings. One thing led to another, and all of a sudden Taudry told me that we had to get married because she was in the "family way." I didn't really understand what all of this meant.

I was about to go on a tour with Ray Shep, so I told him I was going to be gone for sometime and wanted to marry Taudry right away. He didn't know she was pregnant, at least we didn't say anything. We were married in March 1935. Taudry dropped out of school and stayed at home. I dropped out too. Our son, Thomas James Evans, was born that September while I was away on tour.

When I came home and they put little Tommy in my arms, he promptly peed on me. We all eventually moved in with Taudry's aunt Carrie, who had a big house. After a while, we rented a house on Belmont Street.

I might as well confess that before long, I was back on the road again. Music and musicians were my closest family, for decades to come. Being on the road eventually caused strains at home with Taudry and Tommy. After we moved to New York, I always called home and sent money for living expenses, but my frequent absence created conflicts that ultimately led to our estrangement. My one consolation was that Taudry's brother, Clayton, was in New York, so Taudry and Tommy had a familiar face from Pensacola. I admit I used Clayton's being in New York as a justification for my being away so much.

By the early 1950s there was big trouble on the home front back in New York. Tommy was in a special high school that had an emphasis on aeronautic training. During my absence he convinced his mother to let him switch to Spanish so he could be a language interpreter. That led to a big blowout between Taudry and me. I told him there were more than enough Spanish-speaking people in New York, but not enough black aeronautic-trained specialists. Later that year he wanted to drop out of school altogether. We had a big argument about that, and I went to see his counselor, who was not very encouraging. The counselor said when kids make up their minds, as Tommy apparently had, it was best to let them do what they wanted. I asked the counselor if he had any children and would he allow them to make such a decision. I recall his answer's being evasive. Anyway, Tommy and I reached a compromise after a lot of head-knocking. If he stopped going to school he'd have to join the service. I suggested the air force, because I had spoken to my childhood friend and then air force lieutenant Chappie James, who promised to look out for him. Tommy didn't stay in the service long enough for Chappie to do anything for him though. When he came back to the East Coast he got married.

By that time, Taudry and I were on bad terms, and we separated. I thought she was going back to Florida and she may have, but I think she came back to New York. She was eventually institutionalized for emotional disturbance. I saw her a few times there at the facility, but I understand that she was taken back to Florida. I never saw her again. Although we had already been apart for years, we were formally divorced in the early 1960s. Taudry died in 2002. I had always felt some guilt about Taudry. But in those years I was music crazy. There was room for little else.

• • • • •

During the 1930s, white musicians in Pensacola had a union headed by a guy named Tony Bruno. When we played white clubs, the naval base, or dances, the white union guys would come around and ask us if we had union cards. Since we didn't, Shep decided that we should start our own black union. In 1936 or 1937, we had enough members in the band, so Shep wrote the president of the American Federation of Musicians in Chicago. I believe his name was James Petrillo. Petrillo sent us all of our material with the official seal and union cards. We became charter members of Local 548 of the AFM in Pensacola. As a black local, we solicited other black musicians in the area to join our union. By the time I left Pensacola for New York, Local 548 had more than tripled in size. I believe it is still active or may have merged with the white local.

Thereafter, when a traveling black band came into our territory, we had one of our delegates go to the event based on how many musicians they had. We kept a part of the taxes and sent the rest to the AFM national headquarters.

The greatest learning experience I had with Shep was the touring. We eventually got a white booking agent named Brownie Robinson to set up our playing dates. He also booked for the Sunset Royal Entertainers. He was a fast-moving guy. Brownie booked us to play at black dances in a town during the week. Then he would contact a local white businessman.

"Look, this band is going to be open on Saturday, I can let you have them for a good price," he'd say. Since we were already in the area, Brownie convinced promoters that they were saving on travel and accommodation expenses.

Sometimes Brownie worked out a percentage clause for us, which meant that we would get 60 percent of the overall take of a given dance. Sometimes that worked to our advantage and other times it didn't. The dance promoters sometimes specified in the contract that the band would arrive at least four hours before the scheduled performance. This ensured that the dance would start at the advertised time or that the leader could appear on the radio with the promoter to talk up the event. Some of our contracts required Shep, as the leader, to show up at a popular restaurant in the town before the event. He usually had one or two musicians with him to play something. Again, this was for promotional purposes.

The dances were in halls like the Pythias Temple or an Elks Rest or a Masonic lodge. Some held small groups like four or five hundred. Some handled more than one thousand. When we gave a dance in Pensacola, we would rent the hall and charge $1.50 for people to come in. Sometimes we could get as many as fifteen hundred people in the hall and make a couple of thousand dollars.

There were dates when only a few people showed up. The guys in the band called that a "ham job." We'd be playing around ten at night and there would be five or six people in the hall. One of members would start to sniff aloud and say, "I smell ham," or the following day someone would say, "We had ham last night." Once or twice when we thought that the dance would be a ham night, people would start to flock in around eleven at night, especially on the weekends. After paying our expenses, we divided the money up among the band. Everybody got an equal share, including Shep. At the time, the leader got what was called a leader's fee, which was double that of the other band members. Shep was certainly entitled to it because he wrote all of the music, did the arranging, sang, and played clarinet and saxophone in the band. At the time, I wasn't real interested in the business aspect of things. Shep knew how it worked and that was good enough for me.

chapter four

"Ma" Rainey's Deep South

As the youngest members of the Ray Shep band, Bobby Johnson and I got to be pretty close. In the Shep organization, everybody was supposed to be equal. Everybody got the same salary. But when it came to discussing business, it was a different story. One day, the band members were talking about adding another performance to our schedule, and I chimed in, "I think we should forget about that and should . . ."

"You think!?" snapped Mr. Joe Jessie. "Shut your damn mouth! You ain't think nothin'. You ain't even stop wettin' the bed yet. Get over in that corner and keep your damn mouth shut when grownups are talking."

Bobby, my regular partner, and I moved straight to the corner and then made our way outside. I complained to Bobby, "We're supposed to be in the talk, too."

"Don't pay it no mind, Joe," he said. "We'll find out what went on." Shep never treated us like that.

Traveling with a territory band was a hassle, but worth it for the sheer excitement. One night we had a date in Meridian, Mississippi, and Joseph "King" Oliver was also playing in town. He was famous for his brass mutes and had a much bigger name band. We finished playing our engagement early, so I ran to the hall to see this great musician live. He had about seven musicians in his group. Somehow I managed to get down front so I could get a good look because I had heard so much about him. I noticed something wrong with his eye. During a break in the show, he was signing autographs and I got a chance to meet him. He died just a few years afterwards. When I was with Louis Armstrong some years later, he always spoke admiringly of King Oliver, his teacher and mentor.

· · · · ·

A short, stocky woman with her head wrapped in a scarf knocked on the door of our bus, and Toots Singleton, the driver, let her on.

"Y'all know me? I'm 'Ma' Rainey," she said. Her voice was as deep as a man's.

We were making an early-morning stop in Columbus, Georgia, during the late 1930s. We had traveled throughout the night and arrived around six in the morning in the black area of town.

Vernon Barnett volunteered immediately with a smile, "Yeah, I know you!" Some of the older members who obviously knew who she was got out of their seats and began moving toward her. That's when I started to pay attention to what was being said. Her face was roundish with wide eyes and a gap in her teeth. A few of those had gold caps on them.

"Where y'all playin'?" she asked.

"We're playin' a dance here in town."

"Oh, I didn't know about it," she said. The older band members were standing around, grinning like schoolboys. Even Mr. Joe Jessie was standing there showing all the teeth he had and those missing spaces too. I had never seen him act this way. "Ma" Rainey stood in the center of the group enjoying it all. Some of the band members started telling her about the cities and halls where they had played, and each time she said, "Yeah, I played there too," and told them a story about the people or managers there. She told them what she was currently doing, too.

"Most of the time I'm staying home. You know how it is when show business gets in the blood, it's hard to get it out," she said.

She talked about a half hour. At the time, I had no idea who she was, but the older members of the group were lit up by this chance encounter. They began telling us about some of her escapades, and where they had seen her perform, and that she was one of the greatest blues singers who had ever lived. Some said she was better than Bessie Smith. That gave me a reference because I had heard Bessie as a child and remembered the sensation she caused when she was in Pensacola.

* * * * *

Since Pensacola was so close to southern Alabama, the Shep band played in that state quite a bit. During those days there was no telling what kind of welcome we'd get or how the band would respond to it. For example, Toots Singleton was as crazy as hell. He didn't give a damn about how he spoke to white people, and in those days that could easily get you killed. Once he stopped outside of Brewton, Alabama, at a store with a gas tank outside. I was sitting next to a window and noticed sitting at an old courthouse in the center of town a bunch of white men in overalls. They looked like hillbillies. They probably didn't have jobs and were just hanging around with nothing to do. One of them had a shotgun.

"I don't think I would stop here if I were you all," I said to no one in particular.

Mr. Joe Jessie, who was sitting in the seat across from me, turned to me and took up his usual refrain, "You don't think you would stop in there? Shut up your damn mouth! What do you know about thinkin'? You can't find your way out of a telephone booth!" So I shut up. Everyone got off of the bus to stretch except me. I kept my eye on those crackers. They were taking notice of our bus, coming our way. As the hillbillies came closer, I slid down further in my seat.

We had our instruments on a rack on the top of the bus covered by a large canvas. You could still see the outline of the string bass on top.

"What is that?" one cracker said to another.

"I don't know. Them must be band beaters. See the drum up there? I saw a bunch of niggers gettin' off and goin' inside." One guy must have looked up and seen the bass on the top of the bus. "I'd like to see the nigger that can chin that fiddle," he said. The others chuckled. At that point, I slid down under the seat in front of me. Another one said, "It could be a baseball team."

"No, them's band beaters," another one said. "Let's make them niggers play."

Toots was the first one out of the store. He paid the attendant for the gas and got on the bus. I stuck my head up a little trying to whisper to him, but one of those white guys walked up as Toots was closing the bus with the door handle and said in a very polite tone, "Hey, where you boys headed?"

Toots said, "We're going up to Atmore and we're late."

"Yes," the man said, "me and the boys were just talking and we bet you boys can play!"

Toots said in a slightly more aggressive tone, "Yes, but we are late. I'm waiting for them right now." The group had started getting on the bus. When the last man was on, Toots was ready to close the door when the white guy came up behind the last man on the bus. He said, "We just want to hear you boys play one song because we know you can play." Toots said again, "We got to go up to Atmore and you know the weather's bad. Mr. ——— is expecting us. And we late."

"Can't you do just one song?" he asked again.

Then the hillbilly with the shotgun came on and said, "Now listen. By God, we ain't asking too much of you niggers. We tried to be nice, but we just want to hear 'Dixie.' And we gon' hear it 'fore you leave here and you just as well get it in your heads." He then pulled up his shotgun and cranked it. When he did that, man, cats started to hit the floor and grabbing for their instruments and piling off the bus. Even old man Jessie was moving fast. All of them got off the bus and played an upbeat version of "Dixie."

I was so scared that I got back up under the seat. Toots was just sitting up front saying, "I told them to come out of there and just go," as if he were speaking to someone, but he didn't know I was still on the bus.

When they finished, one of the crackers said, "You boys are good! How 'bout one more." They asked them to play "Turkey in the Straw." Then one of the band members said, "Well, we have to go," as they put their instruments back in their cases. One of the men said, "I wish y'all could stay around, but you runnin' late, huh?" Toots repeated, "We late, we late!" A third man had a gallon jug in his hand and said, "We don't have no money to give you boys, but here's some of the best whiskey made in this state and it's for you." He put a gallon of whiskey up on the bus.

Toots said, "Hey, you give us that whiskey and they'll put us in jail."

"Who'll put you in jail?" the man with the shotgun said. "This whiskey is made by Captain Jack. You just tell anyone Captain Jack gave you this, and ain't nobody's gonna bother you. That's the best whiskey and everybody knows me."

Toots shut the door and put the whiskey on the floor. And as we were pulling off one of the men said, "You boys drink that and stop back through on your way back." We got the hell out of there.

When we got up the road a ways, I noticed that Mr. Joe Jessie kept looking at me out the corners of his eyes, but I never said a word. I think he thought that I was going to say I told you so, but I didn't say a thing. I think he wanted me to say something so bad. I heard him mumble under his breath, "that little bastard." He must have been talking about me. Of course, we didn't stop back through that town.

. . . . .

When we could not find a black hotel to stay at, we stayed in people's houses. Once in Dothan, Alabama, we played a dance and had to stay overnight. The promoter was on the bus with us to take us around to the private homes or boardinghouses.

"Drive by 118 South Gray Street. Now this is Mrs. Jones and she's taking four guys," he said. Some guys volunteered. On another street was Reverend Johnson, who was going to take five. The promoter said, "You have to be on your best behavior here. You can't bring no women in there."

"I don't want to stay *there*," one of the guys said.

We got to a place where they could only take one person. Well, I wanted to go off and be by myself so I jumped up and said, "I'll take it." I went into the back entrance of the house, and a man working with the promoter took me to my room. I washed up quickly and jumped right into bed and slept like a log. I woke up early the next morning, but it was so quiet that I stayed in bed so I wouldn't disturb anyone. When the sun came up I got up and went to the bathroom and everything was still quiet. There was another door ahead of me and something told me to go and see what was there. I pushed open a door and there were a couple of caskets in the room! I pushed open another door and there was a dead man on a cooling board. Man, I ran back to my room and started shoving my things in my bag and got the hell out of there like forty going north.

I went back to the Elks Rest where we had played the night before. One or two of the band members said, "Hey, boy, what you doing up so early? You should be tired after all that playing you did last night." I said, "I woke up and saw a couple of caskets in one room and there was a dead man in another."

"You must have been at the funeral home," they laughed. The place where I stayed was a house that had been converted into a funeral parlor. It damn sure wasn't funny to me.

. . . . .

In the spring of 1938, we had to play a dance in Birmingham, and just outside of the city we approached the Warrior Bridge. Instead of our usual bus, we were driving two large Buicks. Bobby was in one car with Johnny Warren, Vernon Barnett, Willie Miles, and Milan Bates. Cecil Williams was the driver. I was in the second car with Ray Shep, piano player Edwin Moss, bass player Kelly, and a boy we called Andy Gump, after the comic-strip character, traveling a few minutes behind. The Warrior Bridge was steep and narrow with no passing allowed. All of a sudden, some white boys in a flatbed truck sped past our car. When they reached Bobby's car, they screamed some names and cut in close, trying to be funny. But their rear fender locked with the Buick's left front bumper. Within seconds, the car turned upside down and skidded up against the bridge railing, while the white boys' truck went over the top and plunged down a hill, crashing on the rocks below.

When we reached the scene, we saw Bobby's car was turned upside down. Thankfully, no one in the band seemed to be hurt. They had made it outside of the car on the passenger's side and were standing around. I called out to Bobby, "Are you all right?" He said, "Yeah! Those boys cut in on us and turned our car over," pointing in the direction of where the boys' truck went off the bridge.

In those days, no matter how you killed a white man, you couldn't convince the law it was an accident. I decided to go down the hill to the spot where the white boys' truck had crashed. I was scared because the climb down the rocks was also steep and dangerous. When I got to the base, I heard one boy groaning and trying to mumble something. He was all busted up because he had landed on the rocks. Blood was all over the place. I smelled whiskey on him too. About ten feet away lay another boy, obviously dead.

White people began coming from everywhere, mostly out of the surrounding woods. A woman started shaking her head.

"That's a damn shame. All these white boys got kilt and none of them niggers got hurt."

A white man who was standing nearby said, "But they was drunk. You can smell the whiskey all on 'em."

The woman insisted, still shaking her head, "That ain't make no difference. It's kind of strange that they got kilt and the niggers ain't kilt—not a one of 'em. It's just kind of funny. They must have done somethin'."

I got scared as white people assembled at the base of the bridge like flies. That kind of talk could be responsible for one or all of us getting lynched by a mob. I thought I had better get the hell away from that crash scene.

Finally, the state troopers arrived on the bridge. One asked, "Who was driving this car?" A shaken Cecil Williams said he was the driver. The trooper said Cecil would have to come with him down to the station to make a report. At the time we actually thought it was a good idea because

Cecil could have become the principal target of the growing mob. But he was subsequently charged with involuntary manslaughter.

A *white* Greyhound bus driver, coming in the opposite direction on the bridge, saw the whole thing, and came forward to offer an eyewitness account of what he had seen. The district attorney said, however, "Three white boys have been killed and someone has to pay for it. Guilty or not."

We went to the local NAACP for help. We also went back to Pensacola and played benefit dances to raise money for Cecil's legal defense. Before joining the Shep band, Cecil had returned from New York City where he had played a ukulele-like instrument, called a tipple, with a group called the Five Spirits of Rhythm. He also danced and sang. Cecil was originally from Pensacola, which made it easier for us to raise money in his behalf. Despite everyone's efforts, Cecil was found guilty of those boys' deaths. An all-white jury didn't take fifteen minutes to render a verdict. I believe he was sentenced to two years, but was released after about seven months. I remember seeing Cecil after his release and his complexion was very dark, as if he had been working outside on the chain gang. We all knew that any of us could have easily been in Cecil's position.

* * * * *

It amazed me that in all of those incidents Raymond Sheppard maintained a dignity that I always appreciated and respected. Bobby and I were the youngest members of the band, but he always treated us like the others, even though many of the older members didn't always do so. Shep always reminded us that we should be gentlemen no matter what the circumstances and he epitomized that in his own manner. We especially adhered to this code of behavior when we were playing for white audiences. We would be insulted and called names by some of the guests we were playing for, but as far as Shep was concerned, we were representing all black people and were trying to prove ourselves.

Sometimes when we got to the outskirts of a town, he would stop the bus. Everybody cleaned up in order to look nice. Shep wanted us to look like we were big-time when we arrived. And that's what we did. When we got in town and stepped off the bus, guys had on their sport coats and suits. Man, we'd step out and walk over to the hotel or the restaurant where we were playing in style. People would stand around looking and say, "That's a big-time band. They ain't no regular band!" They didn't know that we had just taken off our do-rags and stocking caps and polished our shoes.

Shep was very aware of, and sensitive to, our collective social condition.

He, like many others, was in his own way trying to give whites a sense of our worthiness and to give other blacks a sense of pride. I know that many others shared my appreciation.

Once a week, we broadcast from radio station WCAU, in the San Carlos Hotel. This Spanish-style hotel was very exclusive and very segregated. We never played an engagement there when I was with the Shep band, but the radio station was located in the building. We'd have to go up to the studio on the freight elevator and set up. The broadcast typically ran a half hour, but some could be as short as fifteen minutes.

Blacks working at the San Carlos, mostly as maids, bellhops, and waiters, always deferred to us and went out of their way to make our stay more comfortable. They brought us larger portions of food and found other small ways to express their sense of solidarity with us.

Years later, 1984 to be specific, I returned to Pensacola to receive an award from the Musicians' Hall of Fame and I happened to be staying at a hotel not far from the San Carlos. I walked inside the building to look around to see how it felt to walk through the front lobby. It wasn't the great hotel that it was in the 1930s, or perhaps my subsequent exposure made it seem very small.

· · · · ·

Soon after that terrible experience in Birmingham with Cecil Williams, Shep's band lost my best friend, Bobby Johnson. Hilda had already moved to New York, but when she heard about what had happened to us in Alabama, she very quickly made plans to bring her son north. Bobby left Pensacola on July 26, 1938. When I was seeing him off on the L&N railroad, he promised to stay in touch with me. Every week or so I got a letter from him telling me about his experiences in the city. He began encouraging me to come and join him there. He whetted my appetite by telling me that he had seen Duke Ellington or Johnny Hodges, who he knew I loved, but I was still apprehensive about the whole situation. After all, New York City was the real big-time. There was also a different breed of musician, the cold weather that I had heard about, and I did have a wife and a child.

I talked to Shep about Bobby's invitation, though. Even today when I am confronted with problems, I reflect on how Ray Shep would have responded to or handled such a situation. He told me to look at New York as an opportunity for me, a chance to prove myself. He also said to be on the lookout for pitfalls. In those days I knew that he was really talking about women. What I believe he and the other band members thought is that I would get up there, stay a while, and come back to Pensacola with my tail between my legs. But Shep just said watch out for the cold weather, don't catch tuberculosis, and don't stay out all night drinking. He didn't have to warn me too much about that because I was twenty-five before I had my first drink, and that was beer, which I didn't like. He also said that the musicians in New York would try to test me in cutting contests, where one musician attempts to outplay another. That scared me a little, but I had always been a good sight reader. Eventually, Bobby convinced me that I was as good a saxophonist as any he had seen or heard in New York. So I decided to go, despite my mixed feelings about leaving the one man who had been my teacher, colleague, role model, and friend. Even today, I am deeply indebted to him, although I never saw him again after leaving Pensacola.

Much, much later I learned that Ray Shep and his wife, Stella, had two daughters, both of whom were born after I left. Mitzi Sheppard (now Beck) was born in 1940 and is now living in Texas, while Doris (now Payne) was born two years after that and is now living in Tallahassee, Florida. Shep eventually became the band director of my old high school, Washington High. I returned to play in Pensacola with the Andy Kirk band and the Louis Armstrong band, but those engagements were brief and I was never there long enough, it seems, to see Shep. I guess I just kept putting it off. When I returned to Pensacola in 1984 for the award, "Snookie" Willis told me that Shep had apparently suffered from Alzheimer's disease. He died in 1981 at the age of seventy-six.

part
two

chapter five

New York, New York

In September 1938, I was on my way to New York City for the first time. I had already traveled up and down the East Coast with Shep as far north as Richmond, Virginia. New York City was just about four hundred miles beyond. When I arrived at the Greyhound bus station in downtown Manhattan, Bobby was right there to meet me. We took the subway to Harlem. He and Hilda lived at 143 St. Nicholas Avenue in a relatively large place by New York standards. It was a five-room apartment with three bedrooms. Across the street was the Dewey Square Hotel, and to the left was Minton's Playhouse at 118th Street near Seventh Avenue, where a lot of musicians met regularly.

At first, I stuck so close to Bobby that I could have been his shadow. The only time I let him out of my sight was when one of us had to go to the bathroom. I was just plain nervous about being on my own like this. During the day, he showed me around.

Nothing in my life experience had prepared me for black life in New York City. New Yorkers thought their city was so great, they named it twice. Ev-

43

eryone seemed to be dressed so nicely, even the children. When you came from the South you weren't accustomed to seeing people dressed like that every day. People were not only well dressed, but walking around without any apparent destination, strolling in the park and up and down Seventh and Lenox Avenues.

After seeing several black people driving Cadillacs and a few driving Rolls-Royces, I told Bobby, "New York sure has a lot of lawyers, all dressed up with their briefcases." He said, "Oh, no. Most of these people who are dressed up are janitors or waiters or elevator operators. They may work downtown and that's why they dress up." He pointed to one well-dressed man in a shop and said, "See that one guy there? That's Sweet Jelly Roll. He's a pimp and has sixteen girls working for him. See that one over there? That's Pittsburgh. He has ten girls working for him." Some of these pimps even had white girls working for them, which, of course, floored me. Bobby was a good teacher.

It was clear that Harlemites had a true affection for the place. The running joke was, "I wouldn't leave Harlem to go to heaven." The only effect of the nation's economic depression that I noticed was when I heard musicians talking about playing for house rent parties to cover a whole building. Perhaps it was because I had come from the South where the economic conditions were much worse. The streets in the city weren't that dirty and, overall, people were polite.

In time, I walked the streets at four and five in the morning, coming from a playing job. I could walk from 125th Street and St. Nicholas Avenue down to 117th Street, and nobody bothered me, including the ladies of the evening.

Once, however, as I was going into my building, I saw a white man run behind the staircase inside the foyer. I was a little suspicious. Some of the boys who had brought me home were still waiting outside in the car, so I went back and told them what I'd seen. Two of the boys got out and came in with me. Just to play it safe, they kept their hands in their pockets as if they were concealing weapons. They looked under the staircase, and there was a white man in his underwear stooping down trying to hide. He told us not to hurt him. He was from out of town. He said he'd been robbed, but we knew he had been chased out of a girl's apartment in a setup by her pimp. We hailed a cab to take him downtown.

* * * * *

As an American Federation of Musicians member in good standing from Pensacola, I was eligible for certain playing engagements, if I followed the rules. So I deposited my existing union card with the area local, New York

Local 802, and they issued me a temporary transfer card. The first three months of residency I could only play single engagements with an all-802 band. The next three months, I could play multiple engagements but couldn't travel out of town with the band. In extenuating circumstances, I could get special permission to travel with a band, but it had to be an all-802 member group. After six months I could apply for a permanent 802 card but had to pay the union fee. A union delegate named Peek-a-boo Jimmy made sure everyone adhered to union guidelines. I saw him outside clubs watching to see if there were any non-union members in the band or if other infractions were taking place.

· · · · ·

Bobby played with a band led by a West Indian musician named Oscar Hogan who specialized in waltzes and West Indian dance music. Since Bobby was gone at night, he said that I should go around to some of the clubs in Harlem, sit in on sessions, and get known. Eventually that's what I did, but at first I didn't take my instrument.

On Bobby's advice, I began to venture out on my own to see who was playing what. At first I wouldn't talk to anyone in the clubs I visited. I was a natural introvert, but I got up enough nerve to go around and ask to sit in on playing sessions. That's the way you met people. Everybody carried a little address book and they'd take your name and phone number. After a while, I started getting calls. Gradually, I became more outgoing.

The Rhythm Club at 132nd Street and Seventh Avenue was one of the most popular hangouts for musicians. That's where I used to see Jelly Roll Morton. When we talked on a few occasions, he complained that the musicians in his group couldn't sight-read.

He was a light-skinned guy with Italian-like features, very color-conscious, and was always bragging and always using the word "nigger." In fact, his favorite expression was, "A nigger ain't shit." One of the jokes among the musicians was that while he was on his death bed, barely able to speak, he motioned to someone to hold him up while he uttered his last words. In a whisper, he struggled to voice his final words, "A nigger ain't sh—," collapsed, and died.

To hear him tell it, he was the greatest musician there was. He had been involved in a recording project through the Smithsonian in Washington, D.C., and didn't hesitate to let everyone know about it. "I'm important and a part of history," he frequently let us know. When anyone told him to shut up, he ignored it. He did take some musicians with him to record in Washington, though.

Although the Rhythm Club was a musicians' hangout, many of them operated in cliques that weren't that easy to penetrate. Jobs were hard to get, and people gave preference or referrals to guys they knew.

A guy came in the Rhythm Club and said he needed an alto player for a gig that night. I spoke up and told him, "I play alto," but he said, "Man, I don't know you." He turned me down.

The guy may have been acting out of self-interest, because some musicians would say they could play something and got to the job and couldn't play the music adequately or found it was too complicated for their skill level. I didn't understand the clique system at first, but as I became known as a good sight reader and a reliable musician, things improved.

When I thought back on it, I understood why musicians hesitated to take a chance on an unknown player. Years later, I stood in for the regular first alto saxophonist in the George Hudson band from St. Louis at the Apollo Theater. The regular first alto saxophonist played okay but could not sight-read well enough to play for the other acts that the band was accompanying. In these situations, there was little rehearsal and practice time. The Apollo was celebrated for booing musicians who gave bad performances. Even singers might complain in front of the audience when the band was not playing up to a certain standard. This tactic diverted the audience's attention away from the singer to the band. Being prepared in those kinds of situations was everything. A bad performance could get you a bad reputation, which meant you'd have a hard time getting other jobs.

* * * * *

My first real job with a New York band came through a contact at the Rhythm Club. It was with the bandleader Fess Williams. In the late 1920s, he had been considered in the same league as Fletcher Henderson, Joseph "King" Oliver, and a young Duke Ellington. In his prime he had been a headliner at the Savoy. By the end of the 1930s, however, he was considered an old-timer. He had talked to me before at the club, but I had no idea who he was. On this occasion, he asked me what instrument I played and I told him alto saxophone. He asked if I could play lead, meaning, could I improvise solos, too. I eagerly said, "Yes!" I did tell him I was a transfer member of the union local, but he said everyone at Local 802 knew him and he could take care of everything. The gig was over in New Jersey, a one-day job.

A bus picked us up on the day of the performance to take us to Paterson. We rehearsed until 6:30, which gave me about an hour to get something to eat, so I ran down the street, went into the first restaurant I could find, and sat at the counter in the front. After a while I called the waiter, "Hey, I'm next. Let me have some of those . . ."

The guy interrupted, "I'm sorry sir, we only serve members."

"Members?! I don't see no signs that say that."

"Yes, you have to belong to the club in order to be served. You have to pay dues. We only get enough food for club members."

I knew the man was lying. But since I was in a hurry, I didn't give him any more lip. I just got up and went down the street to another restaurant, had a quick bite, and went back to the theater. The show itself went just fine. It was the only time I worked with Fess Williams, and he still had some of the magic of his former days.

My next break came from Bobby. He asked me to join him in his new gig over in Pine Brook, New Jersey, at a place called the Dizzy Club, near Route 46. The club owner apparently had some underworld connections, because we saw several gangster-types coming in and out of the place. One night at the club, Charlie, the owner, seemed very apprehensive, almost jittery. He seemed to have more bodyguards hanging around the place than usual with their hands in their coat pockets as if they were holding guns. Charlie's fears were borne out. Other gangsters drove by and shot up the front window. The bar area was wrecked, but the bartender survived because he ducked under the bar when the shooting started.

Aside from that incident, it was an okay place to work. Charlie was very nice to all of his musicians. We actually stayed at a house he owned about two blocks from the club. Whatever we needed, he made sure we had it. We stayed at the Dizzy Club for several months earning about twenty dollars a week. Since we didn't have to pay for room or board, that was a pretty good salary.

· · · · ·

I first met Charlie Parker in early 1940 at the Hollywood Club on 116th Street between Lenox and Seventh Avenues. A saxophone player named Aaron "Max" Maxwell, who later played with Erskine Hawkins, was leading an informal jam session, and I had almost gotten to the stage to join when I noticed I was being followed in by a young man who seemed kind of lost.

He asked me, "Man, do you mind if I blow one on your ax?"

"Do you have your own mouthpiece?" I asked. I didn't know his name, but that's the way we did back then. Musicians in some ways were like a small community. He pulled out a mouthpiece and I gave him my ax, which is what we called our instruments at the time because they were our working tools.

This young man began to blow and blow and blow a tune he called "Rose Room." He played about four or five choruses before he let the piano player come in. I looked at Max, who leaned over to me and said, "That cat is something else. He's as busy as hell, ain't he? He's making changes I never heard and then some. He's doing something different."

When the young man finished playing, he handed me back my saxophone and I told him, "Go ahead. Play some more. Knock yourself out." As the night went on, he got even better. The only criticism I had at the time was that his tone was a little thin. This could have been the result of blowing on a soft or worn reed in his mouthpiece. Max said, "If that guy ever comes around here again, I'd like to pick up on what he's doing." We were both impressed and surprised by his playing.

It was Max who asked him his name. That was the first time either of us had ever heard of Charlie Parker. He told me he lived at the Dewey Square Hotel, which was across the street from where I lived. I had actually seen him going in and out of that building, but nothing distinctive made him stand out. He was very mild mannered and not at all flamboyant like Jelly Roll Morton. When he started playing, however, it was another story.

As it turned out, on my next big playing job, I replaced Charlie Parker at Ryan's Rendezvous out in a section of Long Island called Kew Gardens. The club attracted a lot of jockeys from race tracks in the area. The group was led by Cam Williams, a very good pianist. Cam lived in Brooklyn, but the other guys lived out in Long Island. Hank Turner was the trumpet player, Benny Moten (not the Kansas City bandleader, who was already dead by then) played bass, Bob Shoecraft played alto, Johnny Norfleet played tenor, and Charlie Stovall was the trombone player. There was also a boy named Al, who was from Newport News, Virginia, playing alto and another boy named Sam who was the drummer. They were some pretty good musicians. I was amazed that they were as good as they were and had day jobs too. Bob Shoecraft became a celebrated lawyer in Xenia, Ohio.

It must have been Bobby who recommended me to Cam Williams for the job at Ryan's because he was also playing out there, but with some other group. I didn't find out that I had replaced Charlie Parker until after I got on the job, and the other boys in the band started to tell me about him.

Cam said, "You know Charlie Parker, man, he can't never be on time. Man, every night the man came jumping down my throat about him being late. And once he didn't come at all!" Charlie had apparently gone to bed Sunday and slept through all of Monday and came back Tuesday thinking it was Monday. Cam told me he confronted him, "Man, where've you been? The man is gettin' down my neck." Ryan, the owner, complained that Charlie Parker had punched in at 12 midnight and was supposed to have been there at 8 P.M. That's why Cam dropped him and contacted me.

Someone told me Charlie Parker washed dishes at a restaurant. I remember him walking as if his feet were hurting. A few years later when we worked together in the Jay McShann band, he frequently played with his shoes off because his feet were paining him.

Cam paid well and he took care of the other arrangements. It was nice to work with him, and our relationship got even better once he saw that I arrived at least one half hour before we were scheduled each night. I met a lot of wonderful entertainers there, like Babe Wallace, the singer and dancer and onetime leader of the Chick Webb band. There was Arthur Lee Simpkins, another great singer. He also sang opera and had sung with the Earl Hines band.

The only complication with my gig with Cam Williams's group was that it was a nonunion band, and according to Local 802 guidelines, I was not supposed to be playing with them. I don't believe Cam was a member of the union at the time. To make matters worse, I was nearing the end of my probationary period. If I got caught playing with Cam's group, my temporary transfer card could be revoked or my probationary time could be extended. Clubs and bandleaders who defied the union guidelines landed on an "unfair" list published once a month in the musicians' union journal. Ryan's Rendezvous was listed for not hiring union musicians. That meant the union musicians were restricted from playing at this club. But I took my chances. Sometimes you just had to do whatever it took for survival.

One evening from out of nowhere, Peek-a-boo Jimmy, the local delegate who was responsible for making sure musicians were following the guidelines, came up behind me. I immediately recognized him. He was a big brown-skinned guy with conked hair who looked as if he might have been a professional fighter. He saw me with the saxophone case and said, "Hey, don't I know you?"

"I don't think so," I answered shyly, keeping my head down.

"Are you a member of Local 802?"

"No. I wish I was."

"What's your name?" he asked. Thinking quickly I said, "Henry James," but the expression on his face didn't suggest that he was convinced.

"It seems like I've seen you before. Where do you live?"

"Brooklyn," I lied.

"Where in Brooklyn?"

"Fulton Street. Hey, look, man, I'm not working at this club. I'm just visiting. I'm sitting in with this group to keep my chops up." I kept walking toward the entrance of the club throughout this exchange. He warned me that if he found out I was a member of the local, he would bring me up on charges, but I continued to walk into the building. I glanced back and noticed that he had pulled out a book and was flipping through it. It must have been an 802 directory, and he was undoubtedly looking for local member "Henry James" on Fulton Street in Brooklyn. When I got inside, I told Cam what had happened and advised him that if Peek-a-boo Jimmy came by asking who that alto player was, tell him "Henry."

For the balance of my probation, I always checked outside to see who was hanging around before I entered the building. I mused to myself, nobody would have caught Charlie Parker out there because he was always showing up late. A while later, after I was a member in good standing of Local 802, I saw Peek-a-boo Jimmy. I don't think he even recognized me from our encounter at Ryan's Rendezvous. Or maybe he did and just didn't let on.

· · · · ·

Not long before I moved away from Bobby and Hilda's, I got a surprise visit from Roy Lee. He had been working and going to school in Pittsburgh. He had actually been in New York for some time before he contacted me, working as an apartment building superintendent in the Bronx. We talked about people back home. It was like we were young boys again.

He stayed with me in my room. He said he had gotten wet or something and caught a cold, and he seemed a little under the weather. After a few days, he wasn't getting better. Finally, he thought he should go to Harlem Hospital. He was admitted and I went to see him the next day. He didn't seem any worse than he did when he was at the apartment, so I assumed he was being treated for whatever was bothering him.

Two days later, a woman at the hospital called. My brother had died. I was in shock. He just didn't seem that sick. I spoke to the attending physician, who told me he thought it was a case of walking pneumonia that had apparently gone untreated for too long.

I went to the hospital to make arrangements for an undertaker to pick up his body, still not completely realizing my baby brother was dead. This was the little boy whom I saw take his first steps, and protected from severe beatings from Muh. He was now gone.

I called Daddy in Bessemer to tell him what had happened, but he couldn't come to New York because a recent illness had kept him away from his job and he couldn't risk taking more time off. He said I should take care of everything and let him know what I needed. He wired money to me to help pay for the arrangements.

I had a small service at the funeral parlor that Bobby, Hilda, and a few musician friends of mine attended. I felt cheated. I had lost Muh before she had an opportunity to see me gain a modicum of success as a musician. Now, Roy Lee had left. In a certain sense I had lost contact with Daddy as well.

He eventually remarried, but he didn't have any other children. I did travel to Bessemer during the war and went through to see him. Bobby was with me. His wife was a nice lady. When I first went to the house, he wasn't there. She knew who I was and invited us to come in and wait for him. I came back later, and Daddy hugged me like he wouldn't let me go. This was unlike him, but I think he realized I was his only surviving son. Daddy lived another fifteen or sixteen years longer, but that visit to Bessemer in the mid-1940s was the last time I saw him. We weren't really on bad terms, but every time we spoke he wanted me to come to Alabama to live and that would ultimately lead to an argument.

My son, Tommy, later went to Alabama and learned that Daddy had left some land to me when he died in the 1960s. I was too uncomfortable with what was happening to black people in that state at that time to go and claim it.

As I reflect back over my life, I can't say how sorry I am for having lost contact with my father. It was one of the biggest mistakes of my life. I can't imagine how he must have felt thinking that I didn't care about him, and yet it was a situation that I could have easily controlled. Now, if I were to pass any advice to young people it would be to stay in touch with your parents (or parent) because you never know how long they will be around, and regardless of the relationship you will miss them when they are gone. But I developed an attitude that those things I thought I couldn't change, I wouldn't do anything about. As a result, it wasn't just my father that I lost contact with. I'm ashamed to say I didn't communicate with many of my relatives.

* * * * *

Shortly after Roy Lee's death, I moved to a five-room apartment at 235 West 110th Street, close to Eighth Avenue, that I shared with a boy who worked as a waiter on the Silver Meteor train from New York to Miami. He was gone most of the time, which suited me fine. I always stayed pretty much to myself. I made acquaintances easily, but I was very choosy about whom I called my friend and took in close to me. Muh always told me, "You watch the company you keep, because if someone does something and they're picked up and you're with them, they say 'birds of a feather flock together,' and so you go right along with them. If they are wrongdoers or something, and you don't know what they are, or what they're doing, you're going to pay the price, too. So you better watch your friends, so-called friends, and connections."

I always heeded that advice. Even when I was in all these big bands, no more than two or three fellas were my friends. A band might have twenty-three or twenty-five people in it, traveling around, but I'd stay to myself. We'd get in a town; I'd call up and make a reservation at a different place from the group. All the guys would head to one hotel and I'd go the other way, around the corner to another one, and only socialize with them if we met at a party.

For a while, I was in rehearsal with a big band that Roy Eldridge had assembled, but when the gig didn't materialize, I was picked up by Oran "Hot Lips" Page, "Lips" for short. He was a great trumpeter from Kansas City who had played with the great Benny Moten band and had more recently been a member of the Artie Shaw band in New York. Lips was a top-notch soloist with a strong, clear tone. He was from the tradition of musicians who played more by ear than by sight.

Lips paid my union fee so I could get a permanent card, and we began rehearsals in a brownstone at 209 West 131st Street. We called it Johnny's rehearsal hall after the owner, who had converted it into a studio. Each of the four floors was used by a different band.

Page's band was in a different league from the rest. Practically every member could have been a soloist in his own right. Aside from me, the other alto saxophonists were Buster Smith and Floyd "Horsecollar" Williams; the other players were tenor saxophonists Ike Quebec and Dave Williams, trumpeters Joe Keyes and Harvey Davis, trombonists Dan Minor and Vic Dickenson, bassist Abe Bolen, pianist Roger "Ram" Ramirez, and drummer Jack "The Bear" Parker. Johnny Hartzfield later replaced Dave Williams as tenor saxophonist.

Floyd "Horsecollar" Williams, like many other great musicians, didn't get the recognition he deserved. I later had the opportunity to record with him under his name. He was the person who exposed me to slang, like, "That's so nice, hit it twice," "Give me some skin, my friend," "Skin me," "I'm booted, and they're all laced up," and "I'm hip to that." When a guy was a real good player, Horsecollar said, "Don't mess with him, he's an ass kicker." This is how I heard him first refer to Illinois Jacquet, a tenor player who was with Lionel Hampton. Horsecollar would even call me out on the street, "Hey, ass, come here," which was short for "ass kicker." I got used to it. Some people credited Cab Calloway with the creation of jive talk, but I heard Horsecollar use it long before I heard Cab using it.

Horsecollar was what white people called a "big burly Negro," and he didn't care too much for them, either. A white guy could be standing nearby and he wouldn't even know that Horsecollar was talking about him. Expressions like "ofay cat" and "Mr. Charlie" meant nothing to a white person.

I remember our first stop with the Lips Page band was Chicago, at the Grand Terrace, which had just reopened under new management. We also played in Kokomo, Fort Wayne, and Indianapolis. We traveled back to the East Coast by train and stayed mostly in the New England area. In Maine we played at Old Orchard Beach and in Portland. In Massachusetts we played in Lynn, Fall River, and had an extended stay in Boston at Crawford House and a club called the Heatwave. A few years later I played at that same club with Fats Waller, Jay McShann, Don Redman, and Louis Armstrong. Lips was pretty popular in that part of the country because he had received so much acclaim when he was there with Artie Shaw.

As the lead alto saxophonist, I was heard by several good musicians who later recommended me for other big bands. From Lips Page I went to big band after big band, and my reputation grew.

* * * * *

After Pearl Harbor, the U.S. joined World War II in earnest. Bobby and I registered for the draft at the same time, but we were both assigned 3A status because we were married and had children.

Many of the musicians that I played with were called into the service. One night there might be five saxophonists, and a week later we would have lost two to the military. Sometimes the band would be on the road and the "letter" from Uncle Sam had to be forwarded to a band member. In those instances, the guy would have to leave the group on short notice. In one case a government man came to the place where we were playing and informed one of the musicians that he had missed his induction date. He had to leave us that night.

A few guys who were called up were rejected for some reason or another. Some acted effeminate, like they were homosexuals. One of our guys went in for a physical but wore ladies' panties and a bra under his street clothes. Although he swore he was ready to go and join the other fighting men, he was rejected.

Horsecollar was another story. After he left Lips and went to the Savoy Sultans, he ran into trouble when the army drafted him. He refused to take the oath of allegiance and was asked to step out of line and taken to a separate room for questioning by FBI agents. When asked why he didn't take the oath, he responded that there was no need for him to take it since he wasn't going anyplace to fight. The agents began questioning him about his politics, his background, what books he read, and even asked if they could go to his room to check it. He said sure, but he said they better not leave anything or he would bring it back to them. They also asked him if he wanted the Japs or the Germans to take over the country. He told them, "I don't give a damn who takes over the country. The Japs ain't gonna see me with nothin', the Germans ain't, and neither are you. So I don't give a damn who takes it over." One agent said, "If you go through with this, you won't be able to get a job." Horsecollar replied, "You ain't gonna give me a job no way, unless it is holding a broom handle to sweep a floor."

Another agent wrote down everything Horsecollar said and asked him to read the statement and sign it. He read it over and nodded his head in agreement as if to suggest that the statement was accurate, but when he was asked to sign it, he said, "Um, um, um, it ain't gon' be like that." One of the FBI agents, who was a big guy, jumped up in his face and said, "What are you trying to do? Make us out to be fools or something? You said everything that is in this statement!" Horsecollar, who was equally large and muscular, with big bulging eyes, jumped up in the man's face and shouted, "I ain't gonna sign it. You can't make me sign it. The government can't make me sign it. The *president* can't make me sign it. You can't do but one thing, and that is to kill me. And if you kill me, you can't eat me. And if you try to eat me, I'll make you sick!" Another FBI agent came in trying to play the good cop to the first one's bad cop. He spoke very softly and politely and tried to persuade Horsecollar to sign the statement. Horsecollar replied, "Man, I don' told him, I ain't signing shit! Look at me. Take a gooooooood look at me. Do I look like I'm fool enough to be over in some country shootin' at some Germans and Japs that I don't even know and who never did anything to me, when you crackers are the ones kickin' my ass? If I should be shootin' anybody, you the ones I should be shootin' at." Well, that statement didn't go over well with the agents, who promptly placed him under arrest.

While Horsecollar was in the lockup, another prisoner asked him what his bail was. Horsecollar told him, "I hear it's around $100,000." The other prisoner said, "Shit! What did you do? Shoot the president?"

His bail was set at $100,000. Al Cooper, the bandleader of the Savoy Sultans, came and put up the bail money for him. As a compromise, Horsecollar was taken through the entire induction process again, step by step, and summarily rejected as undesirable. He didn't even have to go before a judge or have a hearing. Officially his papers were stamped "Illiterate

Negro." Unofficially, Horsecollar Williams was the very type of black man that the military wanted to avoid. When he told us what happened we reasoned that the government wanted to keep him from appearing in open court where he was sure to repeat his defiant statements. That might have encouraged other blacks to act in the same way, which wouldn't have been good for the military's recruiting efforts.

We used to tease Al Hibbler, a blind singer with Jay McShann, that he was next to go because they were taking everybody. One of the boys in the group asked, teasingly, "Who could Hibbler fight?" "The Germans got some blind men. He can fight them," someone retorted. Hibbler always said, "I'll go, I'll go." The army was taking everybody.

chapter six

Hootie and the Bird

B y 1942, World War II had turned the country's economy right side up again. There were so many jobs around that the comedians joked about how choosy people had become as to where and under what conditions they would work. As a result, bandleaders and musicians noticed an increased demand. With more time and money, people, especially in urban areas, wanted entertainment. Because of the war and gas rationing, however, we didn't have the luxury of traveling by bus to get to all those new jobs.

There were many logistical problems with traveling by train. The schedules rarely conformed to the hours of musicians, and we frequently spent whole nights in train stations or arrived in towns at some ungodly hour. A bus usually took us from the station to the club where we were playing, but there was no guarantee of that anymore. Rooms were also hard to find, even when you made a reservation.

There was also an AFM strike against the major record companies. Very few musicians recorded at this period. Those who did, did so underground, against the union rules. We were paid under the table in cash and usually by smaller companies who saw it as an opportunity to cash in on the major labels' loss. These bootleg recordings did quite well considering the circumstances.

We never recorded under real names, though. Many of these underground recordings featured musicians with names like Sunshine Willie, Bobo Jacks, Mayhem Merriwether, and Mojo Jojo. I recorded under a pseudonym as well; many of us did, including some big names you know. Many tried to disguise their distinctive playing styles, but seasoned musicians often recognized each other's sound.

· · · · ·

The first time I heard Jay McShann live was in fall 1942, when I joined his band. My friend Clyde Bernhardt had just joined the McShann band to replace Lawrence "Frog" Anderson. I had gotten a call from Jay, who told me his first alto saxophonist, John Jackson, had been called up by the draft and now the band needed a good lead alto player. He said "Mr. Cornbread" had recommended me. Clyde was commonly known as Mr. Cornbread because someone had mispronounced his name so bad that it came out sounding like that. Jay offered me the job.

I went to the Savoy Ballroom with my ax, ready to play. Along with me in the reed section was Charlie Parker, alto saxophonist; Jimmy Forrest and Freddie Culliver, tenor saxophonists; and Bo Moccasin playing baritone saxophone. The trumpets were Bob Merrill, Bernard "Buddy" Anderson, and Orville Minor. The trombones were "Little Joe" Baird and Clyde Bernhardt. Leonard Enois was the guitarist, Gene Ramey was the bassist, Gus Johnson was the drummer, and Jay was on piano. His singers were Walter Brown and Al Hibbler.

What was instantly clear was that when you played in the McShann band, you felt it. Jay's love of the blues was so apparent, you couldn't help but enjoy it. He was born in rural Muskogee, Oklahoma, in 1916, but went to Kansas City, which was a major music center, to start his career. He eventually put together a territory band and subsequently established a solid reputation as a pianist. He made the transition to a big band by the late 1930s and came to New York in the early 1940s and gained even greater recognition.

Jay was relatively shy, but he could play like hell. When Duke Ellington once heard Jay on a recording, he commented that whoever that was playing, he'd hire him on the spot. Jay drank a lot, but you couldn't tell it because he was always on time for performances and never displayed offensive behavior. We called him "Hootie" because of his drinking, though. In fact, his theme song was "Hootie's Blues." Another song we played was called "Hootie's Ignorant Oil," referring to his whiskey.

Jay liked a relaxed atmosphere, but all of us were intense musicians when we were onstage. We *swang*. There was a spirit for playing among us in the band, and audiences responded. They danced and danced and *danced!* Sometimes the women would throw their pocketbooks up on the bandstand and scream their approval of what we were doing. The only other time I experienced such intensity from an audience was when I was with Lionel Hampton, years later.

The musicians in the Jay McShann band, as good as they were, were like country boys, in a positive sense. They weren't as sophisticated as the New York musicians, but neither did they show that kind of clannish mentality. In New York, you had to be *selected.* In the South, anyone could show up at your house, unannounced, and still be treated well and offered food. In New York, you could sit in someone's house all day and not be offered anything except a drink of water. But I was immediately accepted into Jay McShann's group and felt like a family member.

Although it had been close to three years since our first meeting at the Rhythm Club back in Harlem, Charlie Parker recognized me right away and acted as if we were old friends from New York. My natural inclination was to be cool and formal as I *was* a "New York" musician, but he was so friendly that I went along with it.

Freddie Culliver was the first to start calling me "Jase." Right away, he helped me to learn Jay's book. For example, when we were playing a "head," which was a musical arrangement made up spontaneously, he told me when to come in and when to lay out. Freddie was a funny cat. He sometimes drank from a bottle of whiskey in one hand with a bottle of ginger ale or cola in the other as a chaser. He alternated from one to the other. Some of those boys in that band were wild. We all drank, but several of us never tried any drugs.

Jay was no disciplinarian, and the band had already left its calling card, as I discovered when we were scheduled to play in Chicago. I went ahead of the group to check in at the Oakwood Manor Hotel on Clyde's advice. A light-skinned black guy who was the hotel manager registered me and gave me my room key. As I reached down and picked up my saxophone case, the manager looked over the counter and casually asked, "You a musician?"

"Yeah," I said dryly.

"Who you with?"

"Jay McShann."

"What?! Give me that damn key back. You ain't staying here. I promised to never let that band stay here again. The last time those sons of bitches were here, someone pulled out a dresser drawer and started a fire in the room because they said the room was too cold. And if that wasn't enough, they started a jam session at four in the morning and disturbed the other guests."

I tried to explain to him that I wasn't like that. I told him some of those boys were as crazy as hell, but they didn't mean any harm. I explained that they were young and I was a more mature musician (by all of three or four years), but he wasn't having it. Fortunately, Clyde arrived and came to my rescue. He explained that we had joined the band in New York and hadn't been with the group when the earlier incident had taken place. The desk manager relented and gave us keys to our rooms. None of the other band members, not even Jay, attempted to stay there.

· · · · ·

By far, the person who made the most lasting impression on me from the Jay McShann band was Al Hibbler. He was like no blind man that I had ever met. A few years later he became more celebrated as a featured singer with the Duke Ellington Orchestra. He sang most of the popular songs like "Get Me on Your Mind" and "I Don't Want to Walk without You, Baby." He occasionally sang blues, but that was Walter Brown's specialty with the McShann band.

Al Hibbler never used a cane to get around. If you'd seen him on the street, you might not have realized he was blind. Before a show we walked him out to the microphone; during the show he made it out and left the stage on his own. His hearing was impeccable. You could never fool him by disguising your voice, which I tried on occasion. When I first joined the band, my inclination was to be sympathetic to Hibbler, but the other band members were anything but sympathetic to him.

"Oh, hell, don't mind Hibbler," they'd say. Charlie Parker even told me, "That son of a bitch once stole my radio." They pushed him out of the way if he was moving too slow and never treated him any different than any other band member.

Hibbler was hardly a pushover, though. He could go toe to toe with anyone and if you tried to put something over on him, you met another side of his personality. One of the band's trumpeters, Bob Merrill, owed Hibbler some money and kept stalling on the repayment. He was already two weeks behind the date that he promised to repay the loan and Hibbler was getting mad. When the band got paid, Hibbler called out to Bob Merrill, "Merrill, Where's my money?" Bob stalled again, saying, "Yeah, yeah, I'll get it to you."

All of a sudden, the lights went out. The next thing we heard was Bob Merrill screaming, "Who's that hitting me?!" Hibbler shouted, "It's me, motherfucka. When you gon' give me my money?" Al Hibbler had cut out the lights, followed the sound of Bob Merrill's voice, and caught ahold of him by his neck tie and was jacking him up. Merrill pleaded, "Don't hit me in my lip."

"I'm gonna hit you all over the place if you don't give me my money, you son of a bitch," Hibbler said as he kept slapping him. Someone cut the lights back on and the others pulled Hibbler off of Bob Merrill. Jay told Bob to pay Hibbler his money right then.

He was just as quick to play a joke. One day on my way into a bar, I saw Al Hibbler talking to a blind peddler who sold pencils, erasers, and belts outside the Apollo Theater. His name was Bill. I was going inside a nearby bar. A few minutes later Hibbler came in with the peddler's cane. Hibbler said, "Now he can walk like a real man."

Shortly afterward, Bill came into the bar feeling his way around. "Has anybody seen that damned Hibbler? He got my damn cane. I was talking to him a few minutes ago and he walked off with it. It's not funny."

Oliver, the bartender, said, "Here's a cane. Hibbler left a minute ago and left it here." Hibbler was there the whole time, of course.

I stayed in touch with Al Hibbler after he went back to New York to join the Duke Ellington band, but his exploits did not stop. By then Hibbler was living over in Englewood, New Jersey. One time he was at the Braddock Bar on 126th Street and Eighth Avenue and overheard some guys saying they were going to Jersey. He asked if they happened to be going near Englewood and if he could get a ride with them. The guys said sure, but they had to make a stop. That stop turned out to be a gas station, which they robbed. Hibbler didn't know what was going on, but he suddenly heard sirens and realized he was involved in a high-speed chase. The police caught the guys in the car, and when they realized that Hibbler was blind concluded that he was the "brains" of the group.

"I was just getting a ride," Hibbler explained.

"Well, you're going to get another ride right to the station," a policeman told him. The guys driving the car confirmed that he was not a participant in the robbery and the police released him. It was in the papers the following day.

A few years ago, I was looking at a documentary chronicling the civil rights movement of the 1960s. I believe it was a sit-in in Alabama where people were being arrested. The police were herding black protesters into a wagon to take them to jail. Suddenly, I recognized Al Hibbler with his hands out, feeling for the door. A cop moved his hands up and down in front of Hibbler's face and when he realized he was blind, said, "Hey, this nigger's blind!" As if boasting to the others, the cop said, "We got us a *blind* nigger goin' to jail here." He put Hibbler in and the wagon drove off. I have very pleasant memories of Al Hibbler. He was a fantastic man.

* * * * *

There was no question that Charlie Parker was a musical genius. In fact, I have never heard a recording that he made that was better than him playing a live performance when he was on top of his game. The spontaneity of his playing was incredible and his timing was equally brilliant. He was quickly becoming a legend for the speed at which he fingered his ax. Most of the musicians of the era remember when they first heard him. The band members were calling him "Yardbird" or "Bird" instead of "Charlie." Jay told me it had to do with him running over a chicken or something.

One night in 1942, Jay McShann was the backup band at the Savoy Ballroom, and Lucky Millinder was the headline band on the main stage. An alto saxophonist in Millinder's group named Rudy Williams heard Bird playing "Cherokee," which was his specialty with the McShann band. Bird played about ten or twelve choruses before he let the band in, and unlike Rudy, who moved around when playing, Bird just stood still with his eyes closed or looked up in the air, oblivious to what was going on around him. Rudy's mouth dropped open.

"Where'd y'all get that nigger from?! Goooddamn! That nigger's playin' all that stuff!" Rudy called out, "Hey, Hibbler, who was that nigger?"

Al Hibbler laughed, "That's Charlie Parker."

"That cat's mad with everybody. He is smokin'."

Charlie's playing was so incredible that he made people stop dancing to come to the bandstand and listen to him play. This was unheard-of at the Savoy Ballroom. When Bird finished the number, Rudy went over to introduce himself. "Hey, man, my name is Rudy. I'm playing over on the other bandstand." Charlie must have been high because even though he shook Rudy's hand, the expression on his face never changed.

It hadn't dawned on me yet that Charlie Parker was a junky. Sure, I knew about marijuana and had even heard of people sniffing cocaine. That drug, however, was so expensive it was out of the reach of most people and you had to have some money to play around with that one.

The main drug of the time was heroin, which we pronounced "heron." It was also called "horse" or "junk." People who got hooked were called "junkies." Eventually, stars like Fats Navarro, Charlie Parker, Ike Quebec, Joe Guy, Billie Holiday, Sonny Stitt, Lee Morgan, Miles Davis, Frankie Lymon, and many lesser-known musicians ended up as junkies. It became common to hear musicians saying, "My habit is down to the ground," meaning they needed a fix. There were a few who were able to beat the heroin habit, but it was a hard one to beat.

Nonmusicians trying to imitate musicians' lifestyles also started using drugs. I remember one young boy who was pretty good looking until he got hooked. After that he had so many abscesses on his arms and legs and feet, he had to wear aviator boots because his feet were too swollen to fit regular shoes. That's what happened to Ike Quebec. His legs, feet, and ankles were so swollen he had to wear those aviator boots unfastened. His ankles looked as if he had elephantiasis. Anywhere there was a vein, junkies used it as a puncture area. They wore long-sleeved shirts even during the summer to hide the needle marks.

We were playing in the Savoy for about a month, and Bird was having trouble even then. Walter Brown came in one night spittin' mad looking for him. We had played three or four numbers, and there was a brief intermission before we were to begin the next set. I was sitting next to Charlie when Walter came up and stood in front of his stand and whooop!! Walter punched Charlie in the jaw so hard, he *should* have been out cold. Bird only smiled slightly, which meant he *had* to be high.

"I *told* you I was gonna do that, motherfucka, the next time you went by my woman's house and told her I said to send me some money by you!" Walter shouted. I grabbed my horn because I knew there would be a rumble, but Charlie just sat there with that silly grin on his face.

Bird had gotten involved with heroin at an early age in Kansas City. He told me he was twelve when he started using it. A "good-time" woman whom he was running errands for called him in one day and told him she was going to make him feel good, and that's how he was introduced to it. Now, Bird was properly hooked. He was shooting drugs, and I didn't know what he was doing. I was even loaning him money because he told me he was sick and needed to go to the doctor. I was so naive about such things that when I saw Charlie shooting himself with a needle, I asked him, "Did the doctor give you your own medicine for you to put in your arm?"

Charlie said, "Yeah, the doctor gave me my medicine to take."

"Yeah? You got a lot of nerve to be doing that," I said. I was so afraid of needles that it was hard for a *doctor* to give me an injection. I was just plain stupid.

It was Gene Ramey who hipped me to what was happening. He told me, "Listen, Joe. Why don't you wake up? Stop loaning that boy money so he can get high."

"Going to get high? I thought he was sick," I said.

"He's sick all right. They're going to get that junk."

"What junk?"

Ramey was looking at me in disbelief as if he expected me, a *New York* musician, to know better, but I had never seen anyone shooting drugs in their arms before. "See that stuff they shootin' in their arms? They're doing it to get high. When you see them nodding, they're high." That's when I began to notice "Little Joe" Baird was hanging around Charlie Parker and was also getting high with him, but he wasn't as hooked as Bird was.

Touring with Jay McShann had its moments. Jay was like one of the boys. He was always good to his musicians and agonized whenever he had a conflict with one of us. The tour started on the East Coast. Our first stop was the Royal Theater in Baltimore, and Ella Fitzgerald was the headline artist. She was booked by Moe Gale, who was also the owner of the Savoy. From there it was on to the Howard Theater in Washington, D.C. We had several one-nighters, including Louisville, Tulsa, Topeka, Kansas City, Nashville, and St. Louis. Then we went to the Midwest, where we played in Evansville, Indianapolis, Kokomo, Minneapolis, Milwaukee, Youngstown, Toledo, Saginaw, and Detroit. In Detroit we played at the Paradise Theater for a week.

· · · · ·

The situation with Bird got increasingly worse as the tour progressed. Jay warned him to stay off the drugs, and he managed to stay clean for a brief time, but eventually he would score again. Our engagement at the Paradise Theater on Woodward Avenue in Detroit brought things to a head. On the opening date Charlie arrived late. After that, Al Hibbler could be seen leading Charlie Parker in the building for rehearsals. Hibbler brought him down to the dressing room area where Charlie got up on a dressing table and fell asleep. Al Hibbler and Jimmy Forrest woke him up when it was time for him to go on. They managed to get him upstairs and take out his horn. They'd get him to his chair on the stand, but he looked as if he was sleeping. He'd wake up briefly and act as if he was ready to play.

During one performance, Jay kept signaling to me to push him to wake him. This had become a ritual where I was supposed to shake him, but this time he was much worse than before. I shook him a few times but he still wasn't playing.

"Blow, Bird, blow," I said. I pushed him again but he fell completely over, music stand and all. Jimmy and I helped him back in his chair. When we played "Summertime" from Gershwin's *Porgy and Bess,* Charlie had a solo. It was like he was moving in slow motion. Somehow he managed to finish the performance.

It seems as if he was high the entire week. Jimmy Forrest was looking out for him when we weren't playing. He was so messed up, Jimmy had to take him to the bathroom and take out his thing for him to urinate. He had urinated on himself several times before that. I believe it was on the Wednesday before we were scheduled to close that Charlie got up on the bandstand and, when it was time for his solo in "Summertime," staggered to the microphone. He only played a few notes. He was playing the same passage over and over. After the third chorus, when it was clear that Bird was completely out of sync with the band, Jay signaled the stage manager to pull the curtain while Charlie was still playing. Once the curtain was closed, they got him off. The rest of the band played until the end of the song. Jay had had it.

"Charlie, you've started using that shit again! I told you if you started back on it, you'd have to go." So Jay fired him without notice, and Bird did not make the final night.

The next time I saw Charlie Parker, I was in Charleston, West Virginia, and he was with the Earl Hines band, playing tenor sax. Dizzy Gillespie was also in that band. I was still with Jay. Just a few years later, Charlie was making records and soon became an American icon as the symbol of be-bopism. He had a club, Birdland, named after him, but his drug addiction ultimately cost him his life in 1955, at thirty-four years old.

* * * * *

As I was nearing the end of my stay with Jay McShann, I had something of a surprise. An old acquaintance, Don Redman, of Fletcher Henderson and McKinney's Cotton Pickers fame, made arrangements to use Jay's band to fulfill an engagement in Boston. Jay didn't have any dates for that period, and Don Redman didn't have a band. So instead of finding musicians to put together his own group, he just fronted Jay's band. That's how bandleaders helped each other out. Don turned out to be a good bandleader and a real nice guy. He was a short, brown-skinned, hardworking man who always had a cigar in his mouth. He could compose and arrange like no one I had ever met. He could sit down and within a few minutes turn out something that might have taken other composers or arrangers weeks to complete. Don had made a reputation for composing and arranging for Fred Waring and His Pennsylvanians, Cab Calloway, Tommy Dorsey, Benny Goodman, and a host of others. He was also a real Yankees baseball fan, and it seemed as if we talked more about baseball than about music. At our first rehearsal, he came over to speak to me because I was the only person in the band he knew.

In Boston at the Tick-Tock Club, we were billed as Don Redman and His Orchestra, but we played Jay McShann's book. Thomas "Fats" Waller was the headline act. I never saw such a big man with such huge hands play with such dexterity. His hands moved so gracefully across the keyboard, it was a treat just to see him play. He also sang and used his heavy eyebrows very comically. On top of all of that, he was a cool guy.

Shortly after the Boston gig, I gave Jay my two weeks' notice. It was 1943. Charlie Parker, Jimmy Forrest, Clyde Bernhardt, Al Hibbler, and many others had all gone by then.

chapter seven

The Big, Big Bands

Louis Armstrong was still one of the hottest musicians around. I had known of him since I was a child listening to him on the radio and records. I was amazed to be *playing* with this music legend. Since I was a seasoned musician, I wasn't intimidated, though, just impressed. We called him "Louis" ("Louie," like Louisianans pronounce it) or the more familiar "Satchmo." Although the band paid much better than any I had been in up to that point, it wasn't as exciting as playing with the McShann band. Louis's book consisted of older tunes like "King Porter's Stomp," "Milenburg Joys," "Back of Town Blues," "Struttin' with Some Barbecue," "Leap Frog," and "Sleepy Time Down South," his theme song. Lyrics like "when old Mammy falls down on her knees" and "hearing darkies singin' and the banjos ringin'" weren't politically correct among young modern black musicians like me.

When I played solos, Louis's musicians asked me where I developed my playing style. I'm sure I had picked up some of the mannerisms of Charlie Parker and others in the McShann band, a more contemporary sound than the Armstrong band. Louis's lineup included Shelton "Skad" Hemphill, Bernard Flood, and Hosea Sapp, trumpeters; Joe Hayman and I, alto saxophonists; Prince Robinson and Joe Garland, tenor saxophonists; Max Lucas, baritone saxophonist; Henderson Chambers and James Whitney, trombonists; Lawrence Lucy, guitarist; Gerald Wiggins, pianist; Al Moore, bassist; and James "Coatesville" Harris, drummer.

Louis didn't act as the leader. Joe Garland did most of the work. He rehearsed the band and told us what the schedule would be while Louis sat on the side.

Louis's manager, Joe Glaser, purposely arranged it that way. Clyde Bernhardt recommended me to Joe Garland, a well-regarded tenor sax player who was the music director for Louis Armstrong. Garland had made a name for himself with the composition "In the Mood," which was made famous by Glenn Miller. Joe Garland contacted me after I got back to New York, talking a big salary increase, and hired me over the phone.

He didn't want Louis to think about anything but playing. Louis didn't even buy his own suits. Joe Glaser went to the tailor and picked out five or six at one time and told the tailors, "Make those up and take them to Louis." He had Louis's measurements and everything. He also made sure Louis had boxes of big wide handkerchiefs, and the valet took charge of them. Every night, when Louis Armstrong started to play, the valet put out a stack. Louis held his horn with the handkerchief around it or wiped his face one time and put the handkerchief in a bag.

* * * * *

After one-nighters in Norfolk, Virginia; Richmond; Atlanta; and Jacksonville, we arrived in Pensacola. It was the first time I had been back to my hometown since I had left four years earlier. I saw my mother-in-law briefly and some of my old friends, but we weren't there very long. We traveled by a combination of bus and train. Since the war was still going on, gas rationing was still the order of the day.

From Pensacola, we headed to a military base outside Mobile, Alabama, called Brooklyn Field. The government arranged for our transportation when we were entertaining troops on military facilities and the band was housed on the base. It was common for us to perform for segregated audiences at that time, and the military was no exception. On this occasion, Louis played a dance for the white enlisted men and their dates. A white officer came to Louis and asked if the band could stay a little longer and play a second program for the colored soldiers. Louis said okay.

Some of the black soldiers, however, found out about the "second" concert and put together a delegation to meet with Louis. I was also at the meeting. The spokesman told him, "Mr. Armstrong, we don't mean you any disrespect, but we feel that we are all soldiers. We have to fight the same way, and participate like anyone else. We should have had the same opportunity to be at the dance like everyone else. Please don't feel bad, but we don't intend to show up for the concert. We didn't want you to feel slighted." Louis was diplomatic and said, "Okay. I see where you're coming from. No problem." Somehow higher-ranking officers found out about the planned boycott. It was obvious to us in the band that it had to be a snitch within the black ranks who told the higher-ranking officers because they knew about the planned action right away. They were even able to isolate the "ring leaders" of the planned boycott who had come to see Louis.

Two days later, the military police went to the black barracks, lined all of the soldiers up, and marched them through drizzling rain to the auditorium where the concert was to be held. To ensure that this "captive" audience didn't leave, the MPs guarded the entrances and exits with rifles at the ready. Initially, the soldiers were a little cold. The applause was polite, but certainly not that which the Armstrong band was accustomed to from an audience. Knowing what had taken place, Louis really went all out to make the soldiers laugh by telling jokes about them being forced into the auditorium, and generally creating a light-hearted atmosphere. He had that showman's ability to make this awkward appearance less tense. Eventually, the soldiers warmed up and became quite appreciative and receptive to his performance. The ring leaders were made to sit on the front row. They were the toughest nuts to crack, but they also became more agreeable as the concert progressed. The guards also eased up and let the soldiers come back to greet Louis and the band members without supervision when the concert was over. All things considered, it ended well, but the entire band sympathized with the concerns of those soldiers and we were in solidarity with them.

The next day, I had my own racial "incident." It was at least a near incident. I decided to go into Mobile on the local bus that came out to the military base. Max Lucas asked if he could come along with me. Max was born in Nova Scotia, Canada, and spent his adult years in Brooklyn, so his experience with racial segregation was certainly much more limited than mine or that of any other black man who had grown up in the South. When the bus came to our stop it was pretty full, so Max and I stood a few feet behind the driver. A few stops later, two white girls got on the bus and were standing just in front of me. One of them started trying to scratch her back. Max reached over my shoulder and began scratching the girl's back for her. She looked around, and Max said, "Now doesn't that feel better?" The girl smiled and in a thick Alabaman drawl said, "It sure does."

It didn't really occur to me at first the significance of what Max was doing, but then it clicked. *This son of a bitch is scratching this white woman's back,* I was screaming in my mind. I would have hesitated to do something like that in New York City. *This* was Alabama! The only place worse that he could have picked to scratch a white woman's back in public was Mississippi. My eyes widened, and my knees got weak as all kinds of scenarios started racing through my mind. Would we have to run? Would the woman accuse us of assault? All she needed to say was, "These niggers patted me," or "they touched me," or "they looked at me funny." That could have done it for us right there. I had been careful of such things all of my adult life and here was Max getting ready to cause me to lose it. A middle-aged black woman sitting on the bus, who also saw what Max was doing, put her head down and shook it in exasperation as if to say this poor fool had no idea what he was doing or the trouble he could be causing.

We got off at the very next stop, which was well before I had intended. I looked behind me to see if anyone else aside from Max followed me, especially white men who might start some trouble, and as the bus pulled away, I screamed at Max, "You son of a bitch! Don't you never follow me anywhere! You could have gotten us killed!" He was laughing at me. He didn't know what was going on. When we got back to the military base I told the other band members what had happened and they also jumped on Max for such reckless behavior. We concluded that since Max was so light-skinned, the girl must have thought he was a foreigner.

· · · · ·

On the road, Louis always carried a typewriter. Between sets or playing the theater, he sat down and wrote letters to different people. He typed all the time. He wrote very funny letters—people used to tell me that if they received a letter from him, he would sign it with one of his witty endings, like, "Most Red Beans and Ricingly yours," or "Swiss Krissingly yours, Louis Armstrong," or "Satch."

Louis Armstrong was a big fan of the laxative Swiss Kriss, but that damn stuff could make your bowels run anytime. He offered it to us all the time. If anyone complained about a stomach ache, out came the Swiss Kriss. Once, between sets, Louis was offstage while the band was still playing. We were accompanying another act and when they finished, he'd come back and announce the next song or tune. When it was time to come back onstage, Louis wasn't in place. He yelled to Joe Garland from the toilet, "Hey, Joe, play another number. I'm talking with Swiss Kriss right now. I'm just sittin' on the rocking chair. I'll be out there later, somebody announce the act." Joe Garland would announce the next tune as if he had been through this routine before.

Louis was legendary for his generosity and good humor, but he could display his temper as well. In one incident, Armstrong's road manager, "Frenchie," who had once been his bus driver, could not get the current driver to move the vehicle after a performance because he complained that band members were in the back of the bus smoking marijuana. Frenchie got on the bus and told the driver, "Let's go."

"I'm not moving this bus," the driver said.

"You're not moving the bus?! Why?"

He leaned over to Frenchie and said, "Don't you smell that stuff back there? Somebody back there is smoking that shit. I'm not going to move the bus until they stop smoking and air it out."

Frenchie didn't know what to do. So he went back to Louis, who was grumbling and rolling another joint. The smoke was everywhere. Frenchie leaned over to Louis and told him what the problem was. Louis said in his familiar raspy voice, "What's the matter with him? Has he got the piles?"

"No, he said he wasn't moving until you all stop smoking."

Louis calmly said, "*You* don't have a problem. If he won't drive the bus, you get yourself another bus driver. Just look out the window, there might be one hanging around out there."

When Frenchie delivered the message, the bus driver started the engine right away and sped off. I was saying to myself, "I hope this guy doesn't have an accident."

I toured with Louis Armstrong throughout the United States and Canada. We played all the major cities in Canada including Winnipeg, Toronto, Montreal, and Ottawa. It was my first time out of the country. We got to play every place with Armstrong, but the schedule was grueling. The stress of traveling was getting to me, so I put in my two weeks' notice after about a year. My last job with the Armstrong band was in Chicago at the College Inn in the Sherman Hotel. The band was leaving there to go to California to make a film starring Bing Crosby. Crosby was a big fan of Louis and followed him like he was Jesus. I didn't want to go out to Los Angeles because I would have been gone another eight or nine months. So I went on back to New York to freelance. It wasn't long before I was on the road again with my next big band.

* * * * *

Another advantage to being back in New York was that I could continue my saxophone studies with Louis Arfine, one of the best saxophone teachers in the city, perhaps in the country. I began studying with him after I started in the Lips Page band. Arfine was a brilliant technician, and he helped me to develop my sound dramatically. He was a small Jewish man in his early forties. I kind of stumbled across him, but he was a gold mine. He lived in Long Island but had a studio downtown on West Forty-eighth Street, right across the street from Manny's Music Store. He had me playing saxophone arrangements of technically demanding classical works such as Rimsky-Korsakov's "Flight of the Bumblebee" and similarly challenging Paderewski arrangements. The members in the band immediately noticed the difference in my sound. My calling card as a musician was my reliability as a lead saxophonist and my excellent sight-reading skills.

I was with Louis Arfine off and on for years. He was my principal teacher, but not my only one. When I was in Chicago, I studied with Santy Runyon. He too was an excellent technician, and many other well-known saxophonists sought him out, including Harry Carney, with Duke Ellington; Hilton Jefferson, with Cab Calloway; and many others. He also made saxophone mouthpieces and published his own saxophone workbooks, both of which I used for a long time.

I was in New York for about three months when I was contacted by Andy Kirk. He needed a lead alto sax player. It may have been Jimmy Forrest who recommended me. Andy's group, the Clouds of Joy, had a very solid reputation that was much bigger than Jay McShann's. He had recorded several hit records, including "Until the Real Thing Comes Along," "Big Time Crip," and "Little Joe from Chicago," among others. He had had the legendary pianist and arranger Mary Lou Williams in his group, but she was gone by the time I arrived. I eventually had the opportunity to record with Andy, appear in a film with the band, and play for many of the greatest names in the business while with him.

Andy was a fine man and a wonderful bandleader. He carried himself with class and was universally known as a gentleman. He was from Denver, I believe, and studied out there with Wilberforce Whiteman, Paul Whiteman's father. He went to Kansas City and established a territory band there. By the time I met him, he was a big-name bandleader. When I joined, Reuben Phillips and I were alto saxophonists; Jimmy Forrest, Shirley Greene, and, later, Candy Johnson (who replaced Jimmy Forrest) were tenor saxophonists; Sir John Taylor was the baritone saxophonist; Clarence Trice, "Big" Jim Lawson, Johnny Lynch, and Fats Navarro were the trumpeters; Henry Wells, Milt Robinson, and Gino Murray were trombonists; Laverne Barker was the bassist; Hank Jones was the pianist; and Ben Thigpen the drummer. Floyd Smith played guitar. Floyd Smith was a star in his own right. Andy featured him regularly. On vocals were Joe Williams, Beverly White, and occasionally Henry Wells and me.

Andy lived in the Sugar Hill section of Manhattan, which was a very exclusive area for blacks at the time, at 555 Edgecombe Avenue. Other prominent musicians who were in that building were Don Redman and Benny Carter. Everybody respected Andy. I got to interact with him a lot. If you had a problem, he would always make time to talk with you.

Andy Kirk had a son who worked with us a while as an occasional player. He didn't go on tours or anything but was an even-tempered kid. "Little" Andy was a fine boy and was doing well on the saxophone. He was playing tenor in the band for a while but started fooling around with drugs and got hooked. He eventually died of a drug overdose. That was a tragic thing to happen to a person like Andy Kirk because he was such a good man.

Once we were going through South Carolina en route to Atlanta and stopped to get gas. Andy had given us the go-ahead to use the bathrooms and go inside the store to buy things like cookies, chips, and soda. Several band members got off to go inside, among them "Big" Jim Lawson.

Over in the corner of the store was an old white man sitting on a stool, not uttering a word. Big Jim was looking around. He'd pick something up and put it down and look at something else. The old man got up and said, "What do you want, boy?"

Big Jim turned in the man's direction and said, "Huh?" Whoop! The man hit Big Jim in the head with the butt of his rifle. Stunned and in pain, Big Jim said, "What did you hit me for?" The white man mumbled under his breath, "Tired of these niggers coming from up North and not knowing how to say sir to a white man." By then, the blood was pouring from Big Jim's head and he was holding the wound with a handkerchief.

Ordinarily, Big Jim was a quiet easy going man, but he was clearly angry. He stumbled out to the bus and went to his case where he kept a gun. As his name suggested, Big Jim was no small man. He was going back in the store to shoot that cracker. We tried telling him if he killed that white man, they would get all of us, but he wasn't hearing it. He kept saying, "I didn't do nothin'. He hit me for nothin'." Andy finally persuaded Big Jim that it was more important for him to get his wound treated than going after the man. Andy made the driver pull off. He found a hospital, but the emergency room nurse said, "We don't treat coloreds here."

"Where can we get him help?" Andy asked.

"Try the other side of the railroad tracks. Now you have to leave," she said, pushing us out of the entrance. We got back on a main street and flagged down a boy who took us to what looked like a large army tent. There, a black doctor looked after Big Jim. He confirmed that the hospital that we had stopped at did not treat African Americans, but this cooperative of black doctors maintained the health needs of black people in the area.

· · · · ·

My first big project with Andy Kirk was a motion picture we made with Nat King Cole. He and Andy were close personal friends. When Nat Cole was in New York, he stayed at Andy's place. I remember we filmed the movie in New York, but I don't believe I ever saw it. If I did, I can't remember it. Before filming the movie we had a few dates with Nat Cole in various theaters. Our first one was in Philadelphia in a theater over the Horn and Hardart restaurant. Every show had long lines all the way down the street and around the corner from the theater. The street was blocked off for crowd control. Between sets we would come out and there would be large crowds waiting to get a glimpse of Cole. He was one of the hottest artists in the business at the time. "Straighten Up and Fly Right" was the King Cole Trio's first big success. That was followed by a series of hits with the group, before Cole made it big as a solo artist.

Nat's second wife, Marie, would have food sent to the theater and they would have candlelit dinners. I didn't have the chance to talk with Nat Cole that much because Marie kept a pretty close eye on who was around him.

During my years with Andy, we accompanied several other great singers, including Ella Fitzgerald and Billie Holiday. Many of those artists, like Holiday, Butterbeans and Susie, the Two Zephyrs, Buck and Bubbles, and the Chocolateers, were also handled by Joe Glaser or arranged to appear with Kirk through his contacts. I was featured with the Kirk band singing "Baby, It's Cold Outside" with the girl singer who was in the group before Beverly White. Andy told me Joe Glaser had heard me do it and wanted me to record it with Billie Holiday.

Andy's was the first big band I recorded with. He was with the Decca label. Our sessions were in downtown Manhattan. I participated in recordings featuring Joe Williams and Billy Daniels, who sang mostly ballads. We also recorded a lot of dance music. The first recording in which I was involved with the Andy Kirk Orchestra that became a hit featured the Jubilaires singing "I Know." Amazingly, the artist-and-repertoire (A&R) man didn't want to record that song, but Andy insisted. That was the most popular song from that recording session. I heard "I Know" over the radio and jukeboxes, and the Jubilaires toured with us all over the country. We also toured with the Mills Brothers, another famous singing group that played nightclubs and Hollywood and appeared in several movies. The oldest brother, John, who had been the bass singer in the group, had died and was replaced by the father. I called him "Old Man" Mills.

· · · · ·

I was with Andy on a full-time basis for around three years before I left him to go back to New York. He still called me when he needed an alto saxophonist, but I found the easiest job I ever had in a small, eight-piece house band at the Roseland Ballroom. The Roseland was one of the most famous and long-lasting ballrooms in the country. Many bandleaders had broadcast from there, dating back to the early 1930s. Claude Hopkins, a contemporary of Fletcher Henderson, had become famous for his broadcasts from the Roseland. It was internationally known for its annual dance contest, featuring dances like the Lindy Hop, the rumba, the tango, the samba, and any variety of ballroom dances. We played all dance music. Certain nights would feature certain dances like the tango. It was crowded every night. We played just twenty minutes out of an hour before the featured big band took over. The house band was small. There were only eight pieces. "Fats" Green played clarinet and I played most of the alto saxophone solos. I was finished by one o'clock at night, and that was early by musicians' standards.

I was at the Roseland for about eight or nine months when Louis Armstrong talked me into leaving. Actually it was Ted McRae, who had replaced Joe Garland as music director of the Armstrong band, and Joe Glaser who sent for me. I went down to Glaser's office and his assistant, Miss Church, met me. She frequently smoothed over situations that Joe Glaser had stirred up by cussing somebody out. I was prepared to play hardball, because I enjoyed being at home, sleeping in my own bed. But Joe Glaser said, "You're talking crazy." Actually, I thought he was crazy. He was a hot-headed, rough cat. It was widely held that he had underworld connections. That son of a bitch was rich. He met my asking price, which was *much* higher than scale, and made a few other concessions. In other words, Joe Glaser was not taking no for an answer and I was back in the Armstrong organization. I probably should have stayed at the Roseland.

The Armstrong band's schedule was grueling. We actually played two jobs. After playing three shows at the Roxy Theater on Fiftieth Street and Seventh Avenue, we would leave to play the opening show at the Zanzibar on Forty-ninth Street and Broadway. After finishing the opening show at the Zanzibar, we went back to the Roxy and played our last show of the night. We finished about three in the morning. A completely different group of musicians made up the Armstrong band now. Many of them were younger. Ted McRae was in the sax section and "Fats" Ford played trumpet.

There was a heavy-set guy named Thomas "Sleepy" Gryder, from Cincinnati, who also played trumpet. He must have had a sleep disorder because he'd be sitting talking to you and would suddenly go to sleep. He even did it on the bandstand. One time we were touring and Sleepy couldn't find a room. I told him he could sleep on the sofa in my room. That was one of the worst mistakes I made that night. He stretched out on the sofa, and before I knew it there was snoring like I had never heard before. *Vroooooom.* It sounded like a loud motor. When I couldn't stand it any more, I woke him up. He apologized but after a few minutes, he was back at it. I had to get out of *my* room.

Sleepy's condition also caused some trouble onstage for Bill "Bojangles" Robinson, the great dancer. As the headliner with Louis at the Zanzibar and the Roxy, he always demanded quiet and soft music when he performed because he frequently addressed the audience during his routine. Once, Sleepy lived up to his name on the bandstand and dropped his instrument, which made a loud clang. The sound seemed to resonate much louder because it was already quiet while "Uncle" Bill was tapping. Uncle Bill turned around to see where the noise came from, but kept tapping. All the musicians sat up at attention because Bill Robinson was notorious for stopping the show and telling people to keep quiet while he was performing. That included the audience. For some reason we were spared Uncle Bill's tongue-lashing.

Offstage, Uncle Bill was the most good-natured man I ever knew and could talk like no one I ever met. Sometimes I would try to duck him because I knew I would be stuck listening to him. He usually caught me with his familiar call, "Lil' bruh! Lil' bruh." He always told me what a great dancer he was and about his many accomplishments. Although there were times when I was bored silly, I always let him talk. I think that's why he liked me so much. One night it was pay night at the Zanzibar, and I was walking by after the management had cashed his check. He called me to his dressing room and said, "Lil' bruh, lots of entertainers tell you how much they make, but here's what *real* money is." He pulled out a wad of money that appeared to be about five or six thousand dollars. He began counting one hundred-dollar bill after one hundred-dollar bill. He came to a twenty-dollar bill and exclaimed, "What's that doing in there?," as he tossed it to the floor. I reached down and picked it for him and said, "Uncle Bill, you dropped . . ." "Hold on, lil' bruh," he interrupted, as he kept counting. When he finished, he put the money back in his pocket and was about to leave. I said, "Uncle Bill, here's your money." "You keep it, lil' bruh. Buy yourself some lunch." He drove a Rolls-Royce and frequently gave me rides home.

He would bet on anything. Like so many great black artists, he died in poverty after a phenomenal career.

· · · · ·

I wasn't with Louis Armstrong too long the second time. After the Zanzibar, we toured. But after a few months on the road, I'd had enough. I wanted to get back to New York, to freelancing, and playing single engagements. I soon did some studio work with Mary Lou Williams and Coleman Hawkins on one of Mary Lou's recording dates. The session also included "Fats" Green, Bill Coleman, and J. C. Heard. I was called in to replace Edgar Sampson, who had become famous for his song "Stompin' at the Savoy." Edgar was booked to do a session with Benny Goodman, which had run longer than he had anticipated. Since I was a last-minute replacement, Mary Lou asked if I needed to go over the music. I told her it wasn't necessary. The session went real well.

Not long after, the Cab Calloway band sent for me. They were headlining at the Zanzibar Club. I think the Nicholas Brothers were featured, too. Hilton Jefferson, the lead alto sax player, was going into the hospital for a throat operation and Calloway needed a lead alto player to replace him. I went to the club and told them I wanted to see Mr. Calloway. I was waiting backstage. I went over and introduced myself. Cab looked startled.

"You Joe Evans?!"

"Yes, sir."

"Well, you look kind of young to be able to play my book. I have a pretty tough book and these guys in here are all pros."

"If it's the music you're worried about, I think you'll be satisfied," I said with quiet confidence.

"Well, you do come highly recommended, but with me it's business." He kept looking me up and down as if I was supposed to flinch or something.

Finally, he said, "I'll tell you what. If you can't play my book, I'll have to let you go. There won't be no two weeks' notice. It's business with me."

I said, "With me too. I *think* you'll be satisfied."

"Okay, I'll see you tomorrow night. We hit at seven." He told me to tell Rudy, the valet, to get me the uniforms for the performances and I would start the following night.

I came to the club around six the following night. I was up on the stand talking to Ike Quebec, whom I had known from my days with the Lips Page band. I lined up my music according to the order I was given. I looked it over. It was not as complicated as I had imagined it would be. Cab came on bright and lively and we hit, broadcasting live from the Zanzibar. We started out with his theme song, "Minnie the Moocher," and the band sounded great. We played another song in which the saxophones had to stand up and play. Afterwards, Cab came over and stood in front of my music stand like he was listening to me. He stood there damn near the whole show.

When we broke for an intermission he was just talking, not really to anyone in particular. "Man, I want to tell you something. That is the *readingest* cat I've ever seen in my life! He don't miss nothin'. He reads like he's been here all the time. This cat told me I would be satisfied and I am." Ike Quebec was standing near by and commented, "Well, I could have told you that. Joe can read fly shit."

The caliber of that band was real high and Cab Calloway was known for paying his musicians well. Aside from me there was Rudy Powell playing alto sax, and Ike Quebec and Bob Dorsey played tenor. Al Gibson played baritone. In the brass section were Pops Russell, Jonah Jones, and Shad Collins playing trumpet. Fred Robinson, Keg Johnson and Tyree Glenn played trombone. Danny Barker was the guitarist; Dave Riviera, pianist; Milt Hinton, bassist, and J. C. Heard, drummer. They were all top-notch musicians. I believe Tyree Glenn had to be one of the best trombonists in the country at the time. We played arrangements by Benny Carter, James Mundy, Edgar Sampson, and other first-rate arrangers.

I thought Cab was a high-class entertainer. He was surprisingly knowledgeable about the music, and I didn't expect that. When we rehearsed, the arranger would go over the music with him and tell him what was supposed to happen. He had one hell of a memory. He wasn't particularly close with any of the musicians, although he talked with Jonah Jones and Milt Hinton a lot. He was a fanatical horse-racing fan. He'd lose thousands of dollars in horse races. I was with him in the Zanzibar for about two months while Hilton Jefferson was recuperating from throat surgery.

• • • • •

Although I didn't get to record "Baby, It's Cold Outside" with Billie Holiday, as Joe Glaser had proposed to Andy Kirk, I did tour with her for about three months around 1948. Her husband, Joe Guy, had come to my house to ask me to join his band, and I told him I couldn't. I wanted to stay in town because I was hoping to play in a musical, which didn't materialize. I suggested several other saxophone players to him, but he came back and asked me again and told me how much he needed me. He kept offering me more money. I told him it wasn't a matter of money, but he told me he was in a jam. He said he needed a strong lead alto player because the rest of the reed section was relatively young. He couldn't find anyone else, so I took the job to help him out. He had been a promising trumpet player.

I actually enjoyed that tour. Joe had some musicians in the saxophone section who didn't have much experience, so I rehearsed them separately. We played a lot of southern dates, North and South Carolina, Georgia, and we also played in Louisville, Kentucky. They were mostly one-nighters, but Billie always drew a nice crowd. Her voice was better suited for clubs instead of the big auditoriums. In the small settings, you could not miss the subtleties of her incredible voice.

Billie sang beautifully. She was a world-class musician. I especially enjoyed listening to her do "I'll Be Seeing You" and would eagerly anticipate that song every night. Some of the other songs I remember her doing were "I'm Traveling Light" and "I Cried for You." But one of my all-time favorites was "I Cover the Waterfront." There was something magical about the way she sang that phrase, "I cover the waterfront, I'm watching the sea, will the one I love be coming back to me . . ." She often held that note on "meeee . . ." and the reed section took over while she was still holding it. It was like we were carrying that single note on a cloud of air. I tell you, it was a glorious moment. It was one of those feelings you never forget as a musician.

On top of all that, Billie was always nice to the musicians and we responded in kind to her. Every night she sent a boy around to get our drink orders. When we happened to be performing in dry counties, she'd pay the cab fare for the boy to get to the nearest wet county to pick up our drinks. Her dog—I think it was a boxer—"Mister" traveled on the tour bus with us. She used to hug the dog and treat it like it was a human.

I never got the impression that she liked touring. I believe she was more comfortable in clubs for extended stays. I remember Billie saying, "These one-nighters are a bitch." They were rough because it meant we had to do a lot of traveling.

Joe probably pushed her to go on the road. I thought he was doing it to build his career. He did bend over backwards when it came to the music, though. Whatever she wanted, he did. Billie once told me when we were traveling on the bus that she understood early on how hard life was. Once when she was small she said her mother sent her out of the house while the insurance man came for a "visit." After he left, her mother had money. She came to realize that her mother had turned a trick to get the money. I felt sad for her because she had had such an experience, but I also felt sorry for her that she would say such things about her mother even if it was true.

Billie was a great person. She was also a real kind-hearted woman. All of the harm she did, she did to herself. We all knew she was getting high, even on the bus we were traveling on. We all knew she was hooked on drugs. All of the signs were there. She wore gloves that extended all the way up her arms to conceal the needle marks and all the other things that junkies did to conceal their habit. Those of us who were familiar with her voice knew that when she began slurring her words while singing, she was high. Despite that, she was an accomplished performer. She could take a nothing song and make it a hit. She was a stylist above all. Joe Guy was basically helpless when it came to Billie's drug habit. In fact, he became hooked on drugs himself.

In my experience as a musician, Billie Holiday and Charlie Parker stand out in my mind as examples of that era. Both were great artists. But both had hangman's nooses around their necks. That noose was heroin. It was slowly killing them, and I truly believe they both knew it. Billie was hospitalized once and someone brought drugs to her in the hospital. She had been through a public trial where she was charged for drug use and none of that stopped her. She knew she was destroying herself. Charlie had also tried to quit but went back to it the same way Billie did. He was like a dead man walking. That was a hell of an age.

chapter eight

Call Me "Italy"

Back in New York working the freelance scene again, I was running into fellow musicians at the usual spots. While Charlie Parker was becoming an American musical icon by the late 1940s, his fellow bebop-per, Dizzy Gillespie, was also gaining a reputation. Dizzy and I had met at the Rhythm Club in the early 1940s. I had also heard him at some of those sessions at Minton's Playhouse and Monroe's Uptown House, where I had seen Joe Guy, Little Benny Harris, Clyde Hart, and Thelonious Monk. I think Monk was the house pianist because he was always around.

Dizzy had also sat in with us when I was with Andy Kirk at the Golden Gate Ballroom, which was one or two blocks from the Savoy. Andy let several musicians sit in with us. Dizzy and Fats Navarro were once competing against each other in a cutting contest based on the songs "I Can't Get Started" and "Stardust." Their playing was incredible, with each trying to outdo the other. Dizzy would sit in with anybody who'd let him. In that respect he was like Charlie Parker. They were both always ready to play.

I met the Afro-Cuban drummer Chano Pozo because Dizzy had been promoting him as a fantastic conga player. He had been written about in *Down Beat* magazine. He was a dark-complexioned guy with a full face and an easy smile that he never hesitated to show when he greeted you. He also had very large, strong hands like he had worked in the fields. He lived on 110th Street close to where Bobby Johnson was living at the time. I saw him play with Dizzy at the Savoy and the Apollo. We used to run into each other at a restaurant on 111th Street and struck up a casual friendship. There were many Cubans and Puerto Ricans living in that area. Chano spoke with a thick Cuban accent. We always talked about musicians whom we saw. For example, I knew the tenor saxophonist George Nicholas, or "Big Nick," who was in the band with Dizzy. George played a tenor solo in one of Dizzy's big hits with Chano, "Manteca." We talked about other musicians we played with—and about whom we liked or disliked. Chano always said, "Deezy a greatest musician."

In December 1948, I read that Chano Pozo was murdered outside of the same cafe where we usually met. A while afterwards I was talking to some other Cuban musicians who knew Chano and I were friends. They were telling me they were sorry about my "boy" being killed. I told them I knew about the murder and asked if they knew what had happened. Everyone went silent. The silence was so deadening it was like a scream. They all looked at each other a little nervously before one of them suggested it was a politically motivated killing. One guy said Chano had been killed by political operatives of a Cuban-based group that he opposed. I recalled Chano saying he left all that political "sheet" behind in Cuba and he wasn't going to get involved in it here in New York. As nice as he was, I always had the impression that he had a short fuse and could be quite rough, but he never displayed any of that temper in my presence.

· · · · ·

I also joined the Jimmie Lunceford band in 1948. Lunceford had tragically died of a heart attack the year before, but the band was being led by Eddie Wilcox with the assistance of Joe Thomas. Eddie Wilcox had been arranging for the Lunceford band for some time. He contacted me and asked me to audition for the band. Given my reputation on the road and in the studio, I found that request insulting. He told me he had come across a few saxophonists who couldn't read the band's book, which was difficult. I told him, "Sorry, *no* audition." I figured whoever referred him to me should have also told him I was a first-rate sight reader. After I refused to audition, I thought that was the end of it, but Eddie Wilcox called me back a week later. He said they really needed a lead alto player. We reached an agreement that I would play with the band that night and if they weren't satisfied they didn't have to pay me. I told him if I couldn't play the music I would voluntarily crawl out of the club on my knees.

Eddie Wilcox was a nervous kind of guy. The band was playing at the Savoy Ballroom, and the book was tough. There were plenty of sixteenth notes, modulations to remote keys, and fast passages too numerous to count. It reminded me of some of those training exercises I had studied with Ray Shep so many years before. In fact, the style was very similar to Ray Shep's. When I thought about it, I put together that Ray Shep was with Lunceford in college for a while, and Lunceford's style probably rubbed off on him. After I completed the first difficult number, the reed section started looking at each other and mumbling, "Wait a minute now. Who is *this?* Where you been playin'? Looka here." We played works in D concert, which was B for me (that is, five sharps). At the end of the first set, Eddie Wilcox was beaming.

"Are you satisfied?" I asked him.

"I'm *very* satisfied! Eeeeeverything's gonna be all right. You're hired," he said.

Along with me in the reed section, Omar Simeon was playing alto saxophone. Joe Thomas and a boy named Freddie, whose last name I can't remember, were the tenor players and Dave McRae was on baritone. Trumpeters were Paul Webster, Tommy Simms, and Johnny Grimes. The trombonists were Elmer Crumbley, Russell Bowles, and Arnette Sparrow. The drummer was Jimmy Crawford, and Eddie Snead was the bassist. Eddie Wilcox played piano. Eddie Wilcox, Paul Webster, Joe Thomas, Elmer Crumbley, and Russell Bowles were longtime Lunceford men. Some of them had been with him from the beginning. They were also exceptional musicians, some of the best I ever played with. I toured with that group for several months, mostly on the East Coast. I remember an engagement in Martinsville, Virginia, and we returned to New York for a recording session on the Decca label.

Some years later I was visiting the Jazz Institute at Rutgers University. I had become friends with a boy who worked there who was very knowledgeable about vintage recordings. He played a recording of the Lunceford band for me. There was an alto saxophone solo in one recording and the boy asked me, "Does this alto player sound familiar to you?" I said, "It sounds like Hilton Jefferson." He stopped the record. "No, it's a guy named Joe Evans," he laughed. I didn't recognize myself on the recording. The joke really was on me.

· · · · ·

In 1949, I was approached by this small Jewish guy named Lou Bolton in New York, who told me he was the manager for the rhythm and blues pianist and singer Ivory Joe Hunter. Ivory Joe had recently come to New York from California to rebuild his band. As I later found out, he had fired all of the other musicians in the group with the exception of two. That event turned out to be a forecast of what was to come over the next several years while I was with that organization.

Ivory Joe Hunter was originally from Texas but had gone out to the Bay Area in California, which is where he made a name as a musician. He was at least 6'4" tall and wore thick-rimmed eyeglasses. He was an unschooled pianist and had very little formal education. He had hoboed for some time before arriving out west. I had heard some of his records before I joined him. By the period's standards, he wasn't a strong pianist. He couldn't sight-read well and could barely read and write the English language. He once told me, "Man, the hardest thing I ever tried to learn was to write my name. Damn, I thought I wasn't going to never be able to do it." Some of the musicians in the band ridiculed him and called him stupid behind his back. One guy, for example, would write a name on a sheet of paper like "John Brown." Another one imitating Ivory Joe would come along and confidently read it as "Ivory Joe Hunter." All of this had the culminating effect of making Ivory Joe Hunter very insecure intellectually.

None of that had a thing to do with him as a song composer and singer, however. In those areas he was very secure, if not brilliant. He played the piano with a lot of bravura. It was almost as if he was fighting with it when he hit it so hard. Onstage, he wore bright orange-, pink-, and lime-colored suits. He recorded his song, "S P Boogie," which was moderately successful, but his first big hit was "I Need You So." These and many of his other works did well on the pop charts. He became very big on the rhythm and blues circuit and made a lot of money. If you got along with him, as I did, he could be a very funny man. But that was a big "if," because most people couldn't get along with him. He was nervous and high-strung, and I am sure his excessive coffee drinking didn't help his situation much. He drank coffee all times of the day and night. On a moment's notice, he could become very agitated. Among his other habits was chain-smoking. He mostly smoked cigarettes and always used a long cigarette holder, which he often removed from his mouth in an exaggerated stylized manner. In all of the years that I was with him, however, I never saw him drink a drop of alcohol.

I joined the band in New York. He asked me if I could recommend a tenor saxophonist and I suggested Elmer Williams. Ivory Joe had a seven-piece band, including an alto, tenor, and baritone saxophone. There was also a trumpet and a bass player. Ivory Joe played piano and sang. One of the guys who had survived the purge before I joined was Jimmy, the baritone saxophonist. He was also the music director. Basically, he was a yes-man and did whatever Ivory Joe wanted.

After playing at the Apollo, we went out on tour. We traveled in a large luxury bus with a full-size bed, a shower, a small kitchen, and a few other amenities, heading south to Florida first and then working our way westward.

Ivory Joe Hunter was a notorious womanizer. He always crooned his signature song: "I need you so, to make me happy, / If I don't have you, I don't want nobody else." The women would swoon and fall out. They threw their pocketbooks on the stage and lifted their dresses up to show him their thighs and panties. Ivory Joe loved every bit of it. He had a huge black address book with women's names and addresses from all over the country. More than once I overheard him on the phone sweet-talking women, "Do you miss yo' Daddy, baby? Yo' Daddy will be seeing his baby soon." He'd send for two women and put them up in different hotels in the same town and just run from one to the other. Once he had a woman with him on our bus when another one arrived to join us. While one of the boys distracted the second woman at the door of the bus outside, Ivory Joe passed the first woman out the back window of the bus.

When we got to California, Ivory Joe dropped Jimmy from the band and asked me to be music director. Actually, I was doing the job informally since Jimmy wasn't that experienced with handling musicians. Despite Ivory Joe's temperament, I got along with him very well. I never made him feel self-conscious about his lack of education and musicianship. At the same time, he respected my musicianship and saw that I had a knack for organizing and rehearsing the boys in the band. Knowing his high-strung nature, I also did advance work to check out the places to see if things were set up reasonably before he arrived. There were still those moments, though. If a musician missed a note, he'd get mad. He'd tell me, "These sons of bitches. You pay them money. Man, I feel like blowing their brains out." Finally he came to me and said, "Joe, you be the bandleader. I ain't goin' be bothered with them."

Ivory Joe recorded for the King label, among others, and then went to MGM Records. I remember being in the studio in New York for recordings, but I believe he used a studio band for the sessions I attended. The advantage to being an MGM artist was that they didn't have a race label division and his records went straight to the mainstream distributors. One song, "It's a Sin," had a country-and-western feel to it and attracted large numbers of white followers in the South and Midwest. Many of them didn't know Ivory Joe was black. Another one of his big hits was "Since I Lost My Baby." There was a passage in that song that Ivory Joe sang in and out of a low yodel, "I almost lost my mind." This passage broke audiences up screaming.

His following was large and diverse. Once, we were traveling in Texas when a state trooper got behind our bus and put his lights and siren on. The bus driver was scared because state troopers in Texas could and did stop blacks indiscriminately and who knows what could happen then. When the policeman came on the bus, the driver asked what he had done. The trooper told the driver he hadn't done anything. He had seen the sign on the outside of the bus advertising Ivory Joe Hunter's group and wanted to get an autograph for his niece, who was a big fan. Ivory Joe was asleep when we were stopped and had to be awakened, but he readily complied. He located a publicity photo and autographed it because Ivory Joe Hunter *always* played to his audience and his fans. The state trooper was so pleased—several of us thought that the autograph was for him and not his niece—he escorted the bus, sirens, lights and all, to the parkway.

Although his temperamental outbursts were well known to those in the band, Ivory Joe never let the fans see them. When there was a fan around he held his tongue, but he had no diplomacy when it came to working with others in the business. In fact, he made a lot of enemies. He'd walk in a music hall and say, "Look at this damn piano. Got a fifty-thousand-dollar building and a fifteen-cent piano in it." He'd complain to a manager in a heartbeat. We played in Philadelphia once and Ivory Joe got into a big argument with the club manager over the positioning of the piano. The manager told him, "That piano has been like that ever since we opened this place."

"Well, it ain't gonna be like that tonight! I'm Ivory Joe Hunter. That piano is not gonna be in the corner. It's gonna be out front where I can be seen."

The manager insisted, "Well, I don't see why you have to have it out front like that. Fats Domino played from where it is."

"I don't care if Duke Ellington played it there!! I ain't playing it there."

Actually, Ivory Joe did have a valid point. He was, after all, the star attraction and he was a pianist.

In the nearly four years I was with Ivory Joe, we criss-crossed the country several times. We were busy, too. Here is a sample of what our schedule looked liked for a month in 1949:

July 31	Longview, Texas
August 1	Monroe, Louisiana
August 2	Lake Charles, Louisiana

August 3	Round Rock, Texas
August 4	Dallas, Texas (Empire Room)
August 5	Houston, Texas (City Auditorium)
August 6	Corpus Christi, Texas (Exhibition Hall)
August 7	San Antonio, Texas (Colored Auditorium)
August 8	Abbeyville, Louisiana
August 9	Beaumont, Texas (Chaney Auditorium)
August 10	Temple, Texas
August 11	Hot Springs, Arkansas (Plantation Club)
August 12	Fort Sill, Oklahoma (Non-Commissioned Office's Mess)
August 13	Waco, Texas
August 14	Alexander, Louisiana (Graystone Grill)
August 15	Port Arthur, Texas (West Side Auditorium)
August 16	Baton Rouge, Louisiana; Winstonville, Mississippi (Harlem Inn)
August 18	McComb, Mississippi
August 19	Jackson, Mississippi (Lee Hotel)
August 20	Columbus, Mississippi
August 21	Laurel, Mississippi
August 22	Pensacola, Florida (Savoy Club)
August 24	Ensley, Alabama (Grand Terrace Club)
August 25	Jacksonville, Florida (Two Spot Club)
August 26	Orlando, Florida (Casino Hall Room)
August 29	Tampa, Florida (Watts Blue Room)
August 31	Miami, Florida (Harlem Square Club)

It was like this for a couple of years.

Once, en route to Phoenix, our bus broke down. Ivory Joe decided to charter a plane from a nearby town to fly us to the date. We ended up on two small commuter planes. The instruments and equipment were on one plane, and we were on the other one. As the planes were taking off, a larger jet that was approaching the landing strip nearly struck us. I looked out of our plane and could see the numbers on the bottom of the jet. It looked as if a huge shadow had come over us. The old man who was flying our plane was cussing at the people back in the tower. By the time we arrived in Phoenix, the local television cameras and newspapers were there and set up to interview us about the near-accident. They interviewed Ivory Joe and me. Ivory Joe, of course, played it off and said he wasn't fazed by the incident. He told me later that he was actually as scared as the rest of us, but if he said that it wouldn't be good for his public image, so he faked it. It wasn't until they reported what had nearly happened that I got scared.

By the time I left the band, Ivory Joe had remarried and bought a place in Monroe, Louisiana. His bookings had declined somewhat, so the group disbanded. He was still recording and was concentrating on writing songs, but no major hits came along. Even after I left, we maintained a good friendship for a while and occasionally worked together when he played in New York City. When he and his second wife, Sophie, came to the city, I always tried to see him. We eventually lost contact with each other. He died of lung cancer in 1974 and was heavily in debt, despite all of the money he had made throughout his long performing and recording career.

· · · · · ·

In 1953, I landed my first international engagement. The tenor saxophonist Freddie Mitchell approached me about putting together a group to go to Italy. We knew each other very well because he lived in the same neighborhood as Bobby, and we had played together at the Roseland Ballroom with Ovie Alston. Freddie had also played with Fletcher Henderson and made a name for himself as a tenor saxophonist. He recorded a hit record for the Derby label called "Easter Parade Boogie," a rhythm and blues arrangement that raised his profile and gave him the opportunity to do this Italian tour.

A New York entrepreneur-producer named Charles Gordon sponsored the show, called *The Harlem Melody*. This was a strong show featuring singers, dancers, and popular show tunes I arranged, for the tour, including Gershwin's "Rhapsody in Blue," "Mean to Me," and "Singin' in the Rain." The cast included Corby Alexander and me playing alto, and Freddie on tenor. Willard Brown played baritone and clarinet. The trumpet players were Benny Bailey, Joe Jordan (who had been in Ivory Joe's band with me), and Oscar Meredith. Leon Comegys was the trombonist and Solomon Hall the drummer. Completing the ensemble were Lester Fauntleroy playing piano and Al King playing bass. LaVerne Baker was the headline singer and Laura Pierre was the band's other vocalist. We also had the exotic dancer Flash Gordon and a boy named Jay Smythe who danced on skates. He was advertised as the "King of the Skate Dancers."

We set sail on the *Conte Biancamano,* an Italian luxury liner, in August 1953. Ordinarily the trans-Atlantic trip took seven days, but our trip took eleven because we made more stops.

Our first engagement in Italy was San Remo. From there we toured all over the country. Any town of any size, we played it, including Modena,

Forli, Turin, Florence, Bologna, Bergamo, Reggio Emilia, Rome, and Verona, among others. In places, like Genoa, Milan, and Naples, remnants of devastation—bullet-riddled buildings and exposed parts of sunken ships—reminded us of World War II. We had a pretty good interpreter named Sammy and a crazy Italian master of ceremonies. Once, we found out that he had failed to honor a debt from a previous town. When the police picked him up in the next town, Charlie Gordon had to come up with the money to get him out of trouble.

We were scheduled to return to the States around Christmas. Two of the band members, Benny Bailey and Al King, decided to stay behind in Milan. So when the tour was over, I went down to Genoa with everyone else to embark on the ship for the trip back home. But just before boarding, I decided to stay behind as well. It was a true spur-of-the-moment decision. I went back to Milan to meet up with Benny and Al. We formed our own small jazz quintet with an Italian piano player named Bruno, who was a relative of the former Italian dictator Benito Mussolini, and a Swedish drummer named Stu Erickson. He was pretty good. Playing mostly in nightclubs, I blew at a club near the cathedral in Milan in the same square where Benito Mussolini and his mistress, Clara Petacci, had been publicly hanged a few years before.

Over the next four months I increased my facility with Italian. There were certain museums I hung around so often that I became on speaking terms with the guards and administration. I was also a regular patron of La Scala Opera House, which was close to where I was staying. I saw productions of Puccini's *La Bohéme, Tosca,* and *Madame Butterfly.* I also saw Bellini's *Norma* and Donizetti's *Lucia di Lammermoor,* among several other operas. By coming early on the day of the performance, I could get cheap tickets.

It was a real experience for me. Opera was a genre that I had never really known but quickly grew to love. The singing was fantastic and the Italians absolutely went wild about some of those performances. If the singers delivered a bad performance though, those Italian audiences could be as brutal as anything I saw at the Apollo Theater.

After four months, our jazz group disbanded. Al stayed in Milan, while Benny went to Sweden with Stu Erickson. He eventually moved to Germany. I came back home. From then on, Billy Eckstine always called me "Italy" because I was always talking about my travels there.

Ray Shep.
Courtesy of
Mitzi Sheppard Beck
and Doris Payne.

Joe Evans,
c. 1949–50.

The Jimmie Lunceford band, 1948.

Joe Evans playing with the Andy Kirk band,
c. 1943. Collection of Joe Evans; unless noted
otherwise, all photos are from this collection.

Members of the Freddie Mitchell Orchestra in Italy, 1953.

On board the *Conte Biancomano*, 1953.

On tour with Freddie Mitchell in Italy, 1953.

The Harlem Melody with Freddie Mitchell in Italy, 1953.

The Lionel Hampton band in Hamburg, Germany, 1954.

In France, 1954; Lionel Hampton is at far left.

chapter nine

The End of an Era

When I returned to the states in March 1954, I had to reestablish myself back in New York. Even though I hadn't been gone that long, everything looked so strange. In Italy things moved very slowly. It would take us two hours to eat a meal. I mean, we really sat down and enjoyed it, which included the discussion and the wine. In New York everything was fast. You ate fast, you moved fast, you spoke fast, and you ran fast. That was simply the custom.

I felt better after I joined the Johnny Hodges band within a few months of my return. Johnny Hodges was my idol. As far as I was concerned, on the saxophone *he* was next to Jesus Christ himself. His tone was flawless, and the smoothness of his playing was awesome. You could hardly tell when he was taking a breath. He played a Duke Ellington work, "Prelude to a Kiss," which had a long descending chromatic passage. He did it with such skill and precision, I didn't know where the sound was coming from. It seemed so effortless. It was with Ellington that Johnny Hodges gained celebrity. He broke from Ellington for a while and established himself in his own right. When I joined his group, the saxophone section included Johnny and me on alto, and John Coltrane and Benny Golsen on tenor. John Coltrane and I became very good friends. A few years later when I was working for Ray Charles's Tangerine Records, I ran into John Coltrane in New Orleans. By that time he had his own group and was recording for the Impulse label. I told him I was working in promotions and he joked with me about promoting some of his records as well. The last time I saw him was about a month before he died in 1967. He stopped me in New York on Seventh Avenue and Fiftieth Street. I was producing my own recordings at the time. He asked my advice about buying a tape recorder. I told him to get an Ampex, which was one of the best machines on the market at the time. Emmett Berry and Johnny Grimes played trumpet, Dickie Harris was on trombone and Barny Richardson on bass filled out the Johnny Hodges band.

The headline singers were Billy Eckstine and Ruth Brown. Ruth and I really connected on a date the band played in Port Arthur, Texas. Ruth was singing the rhythm and blues hit "Mama, He Treats Your Daughter Mean." Meanwhile, a woman was standing in front of the bandstand, obviously high or drunk, grinding and twisting away with the music. A man was standing behind her and she was rubbing her buttocks up against his crotch, and he was getting more and more excited. The place was packed with people dancing. I don't think too many people knew what was happening. The man pulled up her dress from the back as she continued to grind and rub up against him. I saw what the guy was doing and thought to myself, "This guy is getting ready to get into something." He kept looking around to see if anyone was looking at him. He pulled out his thing and went to it.

Ruth looked down and saw what was going and got stuck on the word, "Mama, Mama, Mama, Mama . . . ," which she kept repeating. The audience went wild because they thought she got wrapped up in her performance by improvising on the word "Mama" in rhythm. The band kept right with her and they got caught up in her singing too. She turned to me on the bandstand and said, "Looka here," almost about to break out into laughter. I had already seen what was happening. After a few minutes some other guy lifted the woman up on his shoulder and took her out a side door and she was still kicking. Two other guys followed him outside. When she came back in she looked like the cats had gotten a hold of her. Her hair was standing on top of her head. We knew those guys had worked her over or she had worked them over. Ruth Brown and I laughed about that story for years. She and I would see each other and just break out laughing without saying a word.

* * * * *

After being back in New York for a while, Joe Glaser's booking agency contacted me about joining the Lionel Hampton band. The organization spoke the right numbers and the right conditions, so I took my ax to Wildwood, New Jersey. It was the summer of 1954. I joined Hampton's band as a baritone saxophonist. When I was freelancing, I also played tenor, baritone, clarinet, and flute, which I had learned to play after I got to New York back in the 1930s. I played all of these instruments in Hamp's band at some point but, ironically, never played alto saxophone.

That band seemed like a revolving door because there were several personnel changes during my stay. At first, the reed section included Bobby Platter and Jay Dennis on alto saxophone. Jay Peters and Elwyn Fraiser played tenor. Eddie Chamblee replaced Jay Peters and later Ricky Brauer replaced Elwyn. I was the baritone saxophonist. Trumpeters were Wallace Davenport, Nat Adderley (Canonball's younger brother), Billy Brooks, and Ed Mullens. Trombonists were Harold Roberts, George "Buster" Cooper, and Al Hayes. Of course, Hampton played vibraphone and doubled on the drums. There was another drummer named Wilford "Jay Bird" Eddleton, who was later replaced by Rufus Jones. We also had Dwike Mitchell playing piano, Peter Badie on bass, and William Mackel on guitar. The featured singers were Bertice Reading and Sonnie Parker, who also danced.

There was no performer like Lionel Hampton. He was the most exciting bandleader I ever worked with and he inspired the band to reach the same standard. No matter where we were, the audiences responded. I was never with a band that aroused people the way Hamp's did. I think it was his high energy that inspired such a reaction. He'd jump up and walk on the tom-tom drums or on the piano and sometimes on the tables. He routinely tossed his sticks around in the air and never failed to catch them. He sometimes jumped off the stage and marched in the aisles of the theater or club and the band followed him. It was mostly the reed and brass sections that marched with him. The audience occasionally joined in the march. Once or twice he marched out in the lobby and out on the street. He was a real showman. Sometimes we had unscheduled rehearsals just because he wanted to play. He really enjoyed performing. We had several playing dates in this country, and in October 1954 we shipped off on a European tour. The trip over on the *Neue Amsterdam* was enjoyable. When we played for the captain's dinner on the way over, Hamp did his usual and jumped up on the tom-toms, but when he did it, the ship took a dip. Hampton and the tom-toms slid across the floor and he went down. He made it appear as if it were staged, though. He was that kind of entertainer.

Our road manager, George Hart, was a tough street-guy type. George always said, "Joe, if you see me in a fight with a bear, don't help me. Help the motherfuckin' bear." George had a dark complexion and always wore a Stetson hat. He always smoked a huge cigar, and if there was anyone who was a natural gambler, it was him. He sometimes loaned people money to gamble with him. His preferred game was craps.

Well, this large man who looked as if he could have been Sonny Liston's brother spent the entire cruise to Europe in bed in the sick bay. Leroy, Hamp's valet, stopped me with a smile and said, "Joe, come here. I want to show you something."

I asked, "Where are we going?"

"I wanna show you your boy."

We arrived at the sick bay of the ship and there was George Hart lying up in the bed. I smiled and said, "What's the matter, George? The bear got you?"

"Don't make me laugh, man. But I will tell you one thing. Joe, here's my hand to God. If you catch me on another one of these sons of bitches again, I want you to ram your foot up my ass up to your kneecap! If I can't get there by plane, I ain't going, for Hamp or nobody else!"

Someone had brought his breakfast to him in the sick bay, but he hadn't touched it, so I asked him if I could eat it. He waved his hand to say yes. I played with him a little and said, "Boy, George, this sausage sure is good, man."

"Get out of here with that stuff, man. I can't eat no food. I can't even think about eating."

Our first stop was Amsterdam and then on to Germany. One of our stops was the sports palace where Hitler had made speeches more than a decade earlier. We had an audience of eighteen thousand. People fainted. An old woman stood up and was trying to dance and started shaking. She appeared to collapse. The same thing happened to an old man. Several people had to be taken out on stretchers to ambulances. I never saw anything like it in my life. People just went crazy. In Amsterdam, the people jumped so hard the floor started sinking. I noticed the microphone, which was on the floor, was in a different position, but I assumed it was sliding down on its own. Then I noticed the floor was sinking. Gladys Hampton came out and called to Hamp to stop the show because we were playing encores at this point. Hamp just kept going. The managers began switching the lights on and off and eventually shut the lights down altogether. Next, we played in Copenhagen and from there we traveled to Sweden. We recorded those performances live.

In Paris, I met Josephine Baker backstage. She asked where we were going and how the show was progressing and told me she had never seen a French audience respond with such enthusiasm. Every place we stopped, the reaction was the same. The people went wild and Hamp played it right up! We did twelve and thirteen encores. The management would cut out the lights after we played and the people still wouldn't leave. They'd just continue to clap and scream for Hamp, and he complied.

In Tel Aviv, we played at a place called the Ziratron, which was also hosting a circus. They had partitioned the cages with the animals off from the band. I met a rabbi who struck up a conversation with me. He told me how he had read in the papers about the reaction that Hamp's band had received in some of our earlier dates in Europe. He told me that audiences in Israel were more conservative, so I shouldn't be disappointed if the people seemed comparatively subdued.

"It's not that they don't like the music, but they just are not accustomed to showing the kinds of emotions I read about you receiving in Paris."

"Well, I'll believe it when I see it," I said.

At our first performance, Hamp started off with an upbeat tune and he played around on the vibes. The second number he did was a ballad we had played in all of our previous stops. When we began, everyone in the audience stood. Hamp appeared perplexed. As it turned out, we were playing the Israeli national anthem, so the band also stood. It was a real surprise. After that, Hamp struck up a real up-tempo work and things began to heat up. An Arab-looking girl jumped up and ran down to the middle of the floor and started dancing. Then other people started following her and before long the floor was packed with people. They were so excited some police came and settled them down. They continued to holler and throw up their hands.

The loud audience and the loud band set the animals off. We could hear the lions roaring in the background. I looked over at the rabbi whom I had spoken with before our performance. He was shaking his head in disbelief. When we finished he told me, "I've never seen them act like that. I really wouldn't believe it if I hadn't been here to see it." We played our usual series of encores, and the following day headlines in the papers were like, "Hampton destroys . . ." The reaction was the same in Haifa and Jerusalem.

Following my usual custom, I stayed in an area separate from the rest of the band in the suburbs outside of Tel Aviv. It was a tourist-like resort area that had a main hotel and surrounding bungalows. I booked into one of the cottages and it was my home for the next six weeks. It was a really nice place and the service was fabulous.

The first morning I was there, the hotel room service called me to see what I wanted for breakfast.

"I'd like some ham and eggs," I said.

"Sir, we don't serve ham."

"What about bacon? Do you have that?"

"Sir, we don't serve pork here."

Just then, I remembered I was in Israel, the Jewish state. I immediately apologized to the lady. She gave me several choices of meats I could have and one of them was sardines with eggs. That combination turned out to be very good because I had it for breakfast the rest of the time I was there.

I was in Israel about a week when I began to feel bad, like I was coming down with something, while we were performing at the Ziratron. When a nurse backstage took my temperature and it registered over 100 degrees, she said I couldn't go back onstage. I protested, so she confirmed it with Hamp. "She's the nurse, Gates," he said, calling me by the nickname he used for most of the musicians in his band. "Don't try to go against what she says." The nurse called an ambulance, which came to take me to the hospital. After the doctor examined me, he said I could go back to my cottage and rest. I was assigned a nurse who came to visit me at the cottage for the next two days. She took my temperature, measured my breathing, and checked on my food intake. On the third day, the doctor from the hospital came with her. He gave me another very thorough examination and then moved over to the table to write some notes. He said I might be able to resume work the next day if I continued to improve. I asked the nurse in a low voice what all of his treatment would cost. She said, "You can't pay the doctor."

"What? I don't understand."

"When you work in this country, money is deducted from your salary to pay for your medical care."

"Wow! I never heard of that. Can you ask the doctor if I can at least give him something for his wife? He can buy her some flowers." She was initially resistant but went over to speak to him. He smiled, looked at me, and nodded yes. I gave her twenty dollars for him. He seemed somewhat embarrassed but continued to smile. The doctor called me the following morning and cleared me to return to the band that evening. I had never had such care in my life. I wished I had gotten that Israeli doctor's name. I would have stayed in touch with him.

Our trip to Jerusalem a few days later was an experience. We boarded the bus in Tel Aviv and had a full army escort. There were military vehicles in the front and behind the bus. The front series of trucks had these huge spotlights that they shone up in the hills as our caravan moved around the curves of the road.

We were only in Jerusalem a few nights. I remember walking around the city. The scenery, especially the hills, was beautiful. One guy showed me the valley where they took the wood to make the cross for Jesus. I didn't know whether to believe him, so I just nodded my head as if to say thanks. He also showed me where the Last Supper was held. There was a dome-shaped building there at the time.

Lionel Hampton took all the attention we received in Israel in stride. He was used to it. His job was to conquer those audiences once the band struck up. He did his job well.

Although Lionel Hampton was the star attraction, Gladys Hampton was the boss. She was the only person I knew whom Joe Glaser didn't intimidate. Hamp would tell us, "Gladys will be here tonight. You better be on your p's and q's." While we were traveling around Europe and the Middle East, she stayed in Paris. Once a week she'd bring a maid and a butler-like boy named Leo, who also cooked for her, and fly out to pay the band. I remember being in Copenhagen one payday.

"Man, the eagle is flying!" someone told me.

"What room?" I asked.

That day I was the last one to be paid. After Gladys handed me my pay envelope, Hamp told her, "I want me some money too." She immediately said, "What? What the hell did you say?"

"I want some money too. Everybody else is getting some money. I want some too."

"What did I tell you? Didn't I tell you never to bother me when I'm taking care of my business?"

"But everybody is getting some."

She snapped, "Where is the money I gave you last week?" Hamp pulled out a few French francs and said, "This is all I have left."

"Let me see," she said. When he held out his hand, she snatched the money away. "Now get out of here and stop bothering me. If you keep bothering me, I'll cut this damn band down to seven or eight pieces!"

As Hamp was easing out of the door he said just above a whisper, "I ain't cutting it down. I'm thinking about adding some pieces." When both of us were outside, he said, "Give me a cigarette, Gates."

Actually, the cardinal rule from Mrs. Hampton was, "Don't loan Lionel any money because he won't have it to pay you back. And don't come to me saying Lionel owes you some money and expect me to pay it because Lionel won't have any money to pay you." Even though she could be rough, she was very nice to me and I respected her too.

Despite Gladys's warnings, Hamp did get me once. We were in Milan and he called me up and invited me to go out. I was kind of hesitant but he said, "Don't worry, Gates, I got some money. We're going out!" Since I knew Milan pretty well, we went to several places. He spent that money so fast I didn't know where it all went. Then he said, "Hey, Gates, let me have fifteen dollars." I gave it to him, but he was ready to do some more running. All of a sudden Gladys Hampton's warning came back to me and I abruptly ended the night on the town with an excuse.

"I have to go and meet an old friend," I said.

In March 1955, we returned from the European tour to play a big concert in Detroit for several accomplished singers. One of them set the place on fire. She sang!

"Who is that lady?" I asked some guy in the band.

"That's Mahalia Jackson, man!" he said.

Boy, she burned! Oh, man, she cooked! The theater was packed. She sang "I Believe." I had heard her on records, but she was fantastic in person. Dinah Washington was also on the program. I knew her real well. She'd played with us so many times we got to be friends. She knew all of us. After coming offstage she'd come down and shoot craps with the musicians in the basement of the theater. She could play dice with the best of them—and break them. She'd win all the money.

From Detroit, the band went to Cincinnati, Toronto, and Chicago for two weeks. Then we went out west. We played the Moulin Rouge in Las Vegas for three weeks and then went to Los Angeles to record, back on the road again.

•　•　•　•　•

Heading north through New Mexico, I had a terrible headache. We had played in El Paso, Texas, the night before. After the performance several of us in the band went across the border into Mexico. We mostly drank tequila at several bars. The day after, we boarded the bus for Denver. It was October 3, 1955. The World Series was either underway or was about to begin. My head was hurting so bad I couldn't sit in my seat. I got up and stood in the front of the bus and talked to George the driver. Initially I was standing down in the step area at the front where you get on, but my head got a little better so I went back to my seat. It was in the early afternoon, and most of the band was sleeping.

Suddenly, there was an explosion. It sounded like a bomb had gone off. The front right tire had blown and the bus was out of control, skidding along an embankment. George was trying to pull the wheel to the left to steady the bus, but we were going so fast he was unable to hold it. He was almost standing up trying to hold on. The bus flew across a gully and struck a sand embankment. It sounded like another explosion. If I had been standing in the front of the bus where I had just been at the time of impact, I would have been killed.

Everyone woke in general pandemonium. Suitcases and instruments were scattered around the bus. Hamp was thrown completely out of the bus, on top of the girl singer. When the bus crashed, the front right wheel area where I had just been standing had come up in the bus and cut trombone player Larry Wilson's toes off his right foot. People were screaming. I heard somebody scream, "The bus is going to explode!"

I hadn't really moved after the impact. I guess I was stunned. I did feel a large bruise on my head. I looked across the aisle and asked the guy across from me, "Is my head busted open? Am I bleeding?"

"Naw, but you got a knot on your head." I was scared, but I managed to stand up. The front of the bus was destroyed so I moved toward the back exit. I was throwing suitcases and instruments off and someone yelled, "The bus is on fire!" I got off then. All I could think of was running away as far as I could.

I must have wandered up the road, collapsed, and fainted, because the next thing I can remember is a white lady wiping my face with a cold towel. She was pouring water from a thermos on the towel and asked, "Were you on the bus that crashed back there?"

"Yeah. It was an accident."

"What happened?"

"A tire blew out."

"A tire blew out and caused all that damage!?"

"Yeah." I came back to my senses, jumped up, and ran back to the bus. Hamp's ankle was broken, so he couldn't stand up. I made it to Wallace Davenport, the trumpet player, and started to pull him off the bus. He screamed in pain, "Don't touch me! I can't move!" As it turned out his pelvis was broken. George Hart, the road manager, was also busted up pretty bad. Both of his legs were real messed up. He nearly lost one of them.

The driver, George Alliston, was pinned up against the steering wheel. He had to be cut out of the bus. He seemed suspended in the same standing position that I saw him in before the impact. One of his legs was hanging by the skin. He died after a few days.

The accident occurred in between Socorro and Truth or Consequences, New Mexico. Some band members were taken to hospitals in both towns, but the more severe injuries were taken to Albuquerque. Although mine wasn't a severe injury, I also went on the ambulance to Albuquerque. I didn't want to go to either of those small towns.

Once we reached the emergency room, a doctor said, "Oh, God, look at that knot. I better look at it right away." He took me off to a room and X-rayed my head, chest, and wrist, which I had also injured in the crash. He said, "I'm going to prescribe some medication for you and keep you in the hospital overnight because you might go into shock."

"No. I don't want to stay in no hospital," I protested. "I'll just go over to the hotel."

The hotel was near the train station. I ate something and went to my room and fell asleep. I was awakened by another loud explosion. I jumped up and looked out the window and outside my door and didn't see anything. I called down to the desk and asked the woman what the explosion was.

"Explosion, sir!?"

"Didn't you hear it? A loud explosion." She checked with some people in the area, who also hadn't heard anything. I went back to sleep and there was another explosion. I called the desk again.

"You heard that, didn't you?"

"No, sir, we didn't hear it and no one else seems to have heard it."

Then I sat on the side of the bed and tried to recall what the sound was like. Then it came to me that it was the same sound of the explosion I had heard earlier when the bus struck the embankment. I went back to the hospital the following day and told another doctor what had happened. This time I took the prescription.

I stayed in Albuquerque a few days to visit those guys who were hospitalized. Hamp was in Truth or Consequences with a broken ankle. Gladys Hampton and Louis Randall, the band's attorney, arrived, talked to all of the members of the band, and decided that those of us who could travel should return to our respective homes.

I was living out on Long Island at the time. The flight home was very scary. I just kept getting this feeling that an accident was about to occur.

The stewardess had to calm me down. I was even afraid to travel at high speeds in a car for a while after that.

Back in New York, I rested and made a doctor's visit every other week. Once my wrist felt better I resumed my practicing. The band was paid workman's compensation for the time we were off. Since I was well enough to freelance, I did. I played some dates with Dick Vance in Long Island, although technically I wasn't supposed to because we were off for about two months before those of us who could resume did. Lionel Hampton seemed as good as new and was back to his usual stage antics. George Hart was unable to continue with the band at the time. We lost a couple of others as a result of the accident. I think we went back to play in Canada. The band was getting ready for another European tour, but my heart wasn't in it. I put in my two weeks' notice.

Gladys Hampton tried to persuade me to stay with the band. She was reluctant to take a chance with another person for a European tour.

"Is it more money you want?" she said.

"No, I just don't want to go to Europe again." I did manage to find another saxophonist, a boy named Scobel Brown from Atlanta. I took him to Mrs. Hampton to introduce him. She tried again to persuade me to stay. She told me how much she appreciated my being in the band and how she hated to see me go. There were not too many black businesswomen like her. She really was one of a kind. My last engagement with the Hampton band was at the club Café Society in Greenwich Village.

· · · · ·

At first, I freelanced at the Apollo with a small group called Joe Evans and His Bell Boys. Aaron Bell was on piano and bass. We had worked together in Andy Kirk's band. We became like brothers. At the Apollo, we accompanied many popular rhythm and blues artists, including Ruth Brown, Frankie Lymon, Little Anthony and the Imperials, the Skyliners—which was a white group—Aaron Neville, Leslie Uggams, Clyde McPhatter, the Impressions, Big Bill Broonzy, and many lesser-known bands and singers.

I also joined the house band at the Savoy, led by Dick Vance, former first trumpet with the Chick Webb band in its heyday. Balancing my schedule took constant get-up-and-go. For example, I had a boy named Ernie Tanner, a saxophone student of Louis Arfine, play my last show of the night in the Apollo while I zipped off to play at the Savoy Ballroom.

A musical era came to an end when the Savoy Ballroom closed in the summer of 1958, its land taken over by developers. It had been one of the premier spots in the black American music scene for several generations and to perform there was to be the envy of nearly every black popular artist and large numbers of white musicians. With its reputation of being a well-run and well-managed place, troublemakers knew not to act up there. The Savoy was well known for employing some of the best bouncers around the city, many of them ex-prizefighters.

The Savoy was a place not only to work, but also to socialize. In fact, the summer before it closed in 1958, I met a young lady there by the name of Anna Mae Moore. I remember going up to her and asking, "May I have this dance?" When I really got a good look, she seemed very young and very slender. That was the beginning of a forty-two-year relationship. After a few years of real hard courting, she agreed to become my business partner, and my wife.

part
three

chapter ten

The Rhythm and Blues Scene

When the Savoy closed, it was the end of a musical era. I felt a social and economic void. I filled the social void by increasing my time at the Apollo Theater. In order to fill the economic void, I supplemented my income by working for a West Indian businessman who lived in Yonkers, named Steven Hodge. He had been in the United States for years when I met him because he owned Atomic Music Company, which installed and repaired jukeboxes around New York City in barbershops, restaurants, and candy stores. Steve Hodge also owned a real estate company called Global Realty at 275 West 125th Street, just below the Apollo (on the second floor). He approached me about manning the Global Realty office. He suggested that I take a test and get a real estate salesman's license, which I did. Hodge loved money and I brought a lot of business to him. I set my own hours so I could practice and play at the Apollo and a few other places.

I sold buildings all over New York, including houses and apartments, to several musician friends of mine. Hodge taught me the tricks of the real estate trade. For example, I would go into a nice white neighborhood and look for a "For Sale" sign, then knock on a door a few houses away and asked the people, "Is that the house where the Negro family is moving?" Sometimes I'd substitute Puerto Rican instead of Negro. The person would usually act startled or shocked. Some would even admit their neighborhoods were supposed to be covered by racial covenants that restricted sales to whites only. I would then say, "If you're interested in selling your house, here's my card." I listed and sold several houses that way. The practice was called "block busting." It was eventually outlawed and you could have your license revoked or suspended for engaging in it. I also heard of a few instances of imprisonment. I did help to get that office established, though, and picked up more tricks from real estate men all over the city.

· · · · ·

I was actually lured back on the touring circuit before the Savoy closed with Paul Williams in the Biggest Show of Stars tours in 1957. I had known Paul since the 1940s from Detroit. A good alto saxophonist, he switched to playing baritone. He recorded a big hit in 1948, the "Hucklebuck," which also became a popular dance the following year. Older people thought the dance was nasty, but it became Paul's claim to fame. Thereafter, he was known as Paul "Hucklebuck" Williams. He came to New York and established a band there.

The Biggest Show of Stars tours were booked by Shaw Artists. At the time, Shaw had Ray Charles among several other big-name black artists. The tour featured some of the hottest recordings and featured artists who were producing hits. The first tour I can remember featured Sam Cooke as the headline. Jackie Wilson was only one of several backup acts at the time the show was booked. Then Jackie made it big. By the time the tour started, Jackie was as hot if not hotter than Sam Cooke.

Jackie Wilson was personality personified. He stood in the wings of the theater warming up like a prizefighter about to enter the ring. When he hit the stage he was high energy every second, and a thrilling performer. He was so comfortable onstage you would have thought he was born and raised on it. He'd take his jacket off while he was singing and toss it across his shoulder and strut across the stage. He'd fall on his knees and sing on his back on the floor, and similar flashy gestures. The young boys and girls went wild when he did this and would scream and holler. During a performance, he worked up such a sweat he took his clothes off to cool down offstage. When Jackie left the stage, the young people would run out and damn near clear the auditorium trying to get a glimpse of him backstage.

All of this attention had an ill effect on Sam Cooke, who was the head-line act and, as such, followed Jackie Wilson. Sam became intimidated about all the attention Jackie was receiving and even tried to imitate Jack-ie's physical routine, without a great deal of success. Initially, he accused the band of not playing his music with the same vigor that we played Jackie's. I had a talk with Sam and told him that he shouldn't try to imitate Jackie because that just wasn't his style. He had an older, more mature following, and they didn't expect to see him getting down on the floor and being flashy like Jackie Wilson.

"You look funny trying to do that stuff when it's not a part of your char-acter to do so," I told him. The reality was Jackie Wilson was the new kid on the block and Sam caught hell.

I toured with Jackie Wilson later. He always called me "Mr. Evans" and was generally very nice, but offstage he was often high-strung. Once in Birmingham, Alabama, some white girls managed to get by the guards and slipped into his dressing room and hid. When he came offstage and went in, they came out of hiding to ask for his autograph. Jackie walked right back out and told this old redneck policeman guarding the area, "Get them bitches out of my dressing room. They're not supposed to be back here. They know better than to be there." The elderly policeman ordered the girls out.

Later during that same tour we played in Nashville and Jackie was on-stage doing his usual routine. He was near the front of the stage and three hecklers within arm's length pulled at his pants and said, "He ain't nothin' but a little faggot." Jackie obviously heard the remark but kept singing. When the band took over for an interlude, Jackie jumped off the stage, hit one guy in the jaw, and knocked him out cold. He hit the second guy in the stomach and the third guy ran.

"Now who's the faggot? If you want some more, I'll be back as soon as I finish this number," he said, pointing to the guy whom he had hit in the stomach. He jumped back on the stage, kicked the microphone up and caught it, and continued singing. Later I found out that Jackie had been an amateur prizefighter.

*   *   *   *   *

In the fall of 1958, I toured again with another show produced by GAC Super Productions. Irvin Feld was the promoter and Sil Austin was the bandleader. Sil and I were friends from the Savoy. He was a tenor saxophon-ist who had played with the trumpeter Cootie Williams. He had a regular band but had to augment it with more musicians for the tour. This tour was called the Biggest Show of Stars for 1958 and included Buddy Holly and the Crickets, Frankie Avalon, Bobby Darin, Clyde McPhatter, the Coasters, the Danleers, the Olympics, Harold Croomer, and Jimmy Clanton. Bobby Darin and I spoke quite a bit, but they were a bunch of kids as far as I was concerned. I had known Clyde McPhatter from having played for him when he was with the Dominoes. He was a nice boy and very mature for his age.

Those tours were rough. They lasted a little more than a month with thirty-five dates. We traveled to cities by bus and our stops included Dallas, Houston, Fort Worth, Atlanta, Birmingham, and others. It was still segregated, but you could notice gradual changes, such as a few blacks in the audiences in those southern cities.

* * * * *

Global Realty was very flexible with my touring schedule, but I was involved with other business at the same time. I had just come off of a Biggest Show tour when I met my longtime friend, the trombonist Clarence Johnson, better known as Jack Rags. We had been friends since the early 1940s.

"What'cha doin'?" Jack asked me. "Listen, Joe. I've formed my own record label. Since you're traveling around so much, you can take some of my records to be played at the radio stations where you stop." Then he added, "There's a lot of money to be made." He knew that would catch my attention. Jack's label was called Cee Jay Records, but he also owned the Revival label, which recorded mostly gospel music, and he also had a partnership in the Everlast label with Danny Robinson.

I started off doing promotions for Cee Jay Records. This meant getting to know the disc jockeys, taking them to lunch and dinner, and meeting their wives. To put it another way, I was gaining influence with them. I did this mostly when I was out on the road with a band. I soon learned you could form a record company in one room. All you needed was a phone and the influence to get your records played consistently over the airwaves. I went out with other tours, including Dick Clark's Caravan of Stars, and did my usual run to the local disc jockeys to plug Cee Jay recordings. When I came back to New York, I played dates at the Apollo and worked with Jack. I wrote and arranged music for the Cee Jay recording dates, auditioned artists, and helped record them. I also contacted disc jockeys in the New York and New Jersey area to play our records.

At record conventions I made further business contacts. The major association was the National Association of Radio Announcers (NARA), which eventually became known as the National Association of Television and Radio Announcers (NATRA). Jack's mother lived in Baltimore and he had considerable disc jockey contacts there. Through him, I met disc jockeys like Kelson Fisher, Larry Dean, and others who were influential in my breaking into that market once I had my own label.

Jack discovered a woman in Baltimore who recorded the first rhythm and blues hit for Cee Jay. The singer's name was Betty James. Her husband accompanied her on guitar and her son played bass. That combination was good. Jack signed her up and assigned the group to me to record. I set the recording session up in New York. They recorded three or four songs, but it was "A Little Mixed Up" that became big. The record number was 583 on the Cee Jay label. The master number was CJ8174 and was labeled as a Johnson-Evans production. We didn't have much money, so we could only supply so many copies of one record. Jack was scared that someone would come along and "cover" it because we couldn't keep up with the demand. Larger companies could simply cover, that is, get another group or artist to record your work. All they had to do was to write the company that produced the original of the song, requesting a license to record the song and naming the artist or group who would record it. The standard fee for such a license was around three cents per copy of the record sold. If the original company didn't respond, the company wishing to cover a song simply filed a "Notice of Use" and sent it to the publisher of the work. The covering label had to pay the publisher/owner of the song some fee, but they sometimes stood to make much more from recording the song. There was, however, no guarantee of success.

"A Little Mixed Up" sold well in all of the southern markets, including Alabama, Tennessee, Florida, and Georgia, and even did well in Chicago. We eventually agreed to let Chess Records distribute it on their label. Leonard Chess made a reasonable financial offer to take it over. He had an international distribution network, which was obviously much larger than ours. Jack agreed to let Leonard Chess have half of the publishing rights, which was a mistake because it limited our creative control over the material. I believe Koko Taylor came along a little later and covered it. The arrangement with Chess turned out to be a mistake that I never made again.

In the fall of 1961, I went out with Paul Williams on another Biggest Show of Stars tour. This one featured Brook Benton, the Platters, Del Shannon, Dee Clark, the Drifters, the Cleftones, the Jarmels, and a few others. We were in Milwaukee when I called back to New York to touch base with Jack and let him know how things were going. His wife, Edna, told me he had died the day before of a massive heart attack. It was late October and near the end of the tour, so I finished it and then went back to New York. I tried to talk to Edna about continuing the company. I told her I would be doing the work and she'd continue taking care of the books. She wasn't interested and couldn't maintain that activity and her full-time job.

* * * * *

Someone recommended me to Joe Adams, who was the personal manager for Ray Charles. Joe reached me, probably through a disc jockey contact, and asked if I would consider becoming the national promotion director for Tangerine Records, which was owned by Ray Charles. I was based in New York, but Joe and the Ray Charles organization were in Los Angeles. I was basically doing the same thing that I had done for Cee Jay, but on a slightly larger scale and with a larger budget. They were also aware of my writing and arranging capabilities, so I was occasionally involved in music arranging for recording sessions. The first one I participated in was for a singer, Lula Reed, who made a name nationally, but had of late fallen into a recording slump. Ray Charles was trying to revive her career.

By the time I accepted the position with Tangerine Records, I was really liking the record business. I couldn't decide if I wanted to produce and record the songs that I wrote and arranged and place them with a bigger company for distribution, or start my own label. Initially, I tried going to a few record labels like Atlantic, Josie, Twentieth Century, Kapp, and several others. All of them turned down the records I brought to them. So the choice was clear. I'd form my own company.

In the spring of 1962, I went out on another Biggest Show tours with Paul Williams. This one featured Fats Domino and Brook Benton as the headline acts. It also featured the Impressions (with Curtis Mayfield), Gene "Duke of Earl" Chandler, Don and Juan, Marie Knight, the Twisting Parkettes, Harold Croomer, and Bruce Channel, a boy from Texas for whom I wrote arrangements.

I told Paul about my plans to start a record label. He had a strong interest in artist management and booking, which I thought would be an ideal combination. I asked him to be my partner in the company and he agreed. I had to go down to lower Manhattan to the Hall of Records to register the business. There was just one problem. I didn't have a name for the company. I came out of the subway and saw a huge billboard advertising a show with the word "Carnival" boldly printed on it. That was my new record label's name, Carnival Record Company. Our address was

605 West 156th Street, near Amsterdam, which was actually Paul's home address. Edna Johnson, Jack Rag's widow, set up the books for us.

Carnival's first recording was a girl group from Trenton, New Jersey, called the Tren-Teens. They were actually in rehearsal preparing to record on Cee Jay Records when Jack died. Instead of being with Cee Jay, they became Carnival's first artists. They recorded "Your Yah-Yah Is Gone" and "My Baby's Gone." We next recorded a rhythm and blues singer, Delores Johnson from Texas. Delores was in New York and had just left the Ike and Tina Turner revue. I went to see Ben E. King, a producer and composer in search of some new talent, and he told me about Delores. He said I should consider recording her. It only took a few minutes of hearing her for me to be convinced. Boy, she was dynamite! We recorded "What Kind of Man Are You?" and "Try Me One More Time." She was fabulous. The session was done in haste because she wanted to get back to Texas. Had she stayed in the area and I had time to work with her, there is no question that I could have made several hits with her, because she was a great singer. Sadly, I never saw her again.

Along with the record label, Paul and I formed Brightstar Publishing Company to publish the songs that we wrote and produced on the label. I registered Brightstar with Broadcast Music Incorporated (BMI) to ensure that anytime any of our songs were played over the radio we would be given proper credit for them.

Starting a record label and publishing company and recording musicians was exciting and fulfilling, but it wasn't generating much money at that point. There was also another conflict. I was still formally employed by Ray Charles's label, Tangerine Records. That relationship began to sour following an incident in Atlanta. I had the opportunity to acquire the master of a song, "With Every Beat of My Heart," by an unknown group that I thought had great hit potential. A female disc jockey contact of mine in Atlanta put me in touch with the guy who recorded the group. My disc jockey friend told me about the group and how she had gotten good listener response when she played the dub over the air. Because I was affiliated with Ray Charles and his record company, the producer of the song was willing to give me a dub. I was certain that this song would be a hit for Tangerine and even told the singing group and the producer so, but that I had to get approval from the top to move on it.

I was impressed enough to take the dub of "With Every Beat of My Heart" directly to Ray, in New York City. He didn't think much of the record. He said, "You don't want to record that kind of stuff, do you?"

"I'll record anything that will make a hit for the company," I told him. But Ray wasn't impressed, I couldn't get a contract for the group. That was a bitter pill to swallow especially after the Pips, later known as Gladys Knight and the Pips, became national best sellers with that song within one or two months after I first heard them and attempted to bring them to Tangerine Records. I left Tangerine—not on the best terms shortly after that—to pursue my own recording projects.

Around that time I was contacted by the tenor saxophonist Choker Campbell about coming out to Detroit to work with the expanding Motown Records. It was owned and operated by Berry Gordy. I was based in Detroit for about seven months and stayed at one of Berry's old houses with two other musicians. I participated in several record dates for Motown. They recorded around the clock. They had a studio in the building that is now known as "Hitsville U.S.A." We also did live recordings in auditoriums in Detroit and then went on tour as the Motown Revue. Marvin Gaye, the Contours, the Marvelettes, the Miracles (with Smokey Robinson), the Supremes, the Temptations, Martha and the Vandellas, Stevie Wonder, and Mary Wells were all part of those tours. All of those groups became big acts, with the possible exception of the Contours. Their big hit was the upbeat dance song "Do You Love Me?" There was a line in that song, "Now that I can dance," in which each of the members of the group took a turn singing the word "dance." It was always a showstopper with the kids dancing in the aisles of the auditoriums. That was the paradox of the popular music world, because I thought the Contours were as good as, if not better than, the other groups that made it bigger.

We went to the East Coast with stops in Philadelphia, Newark, and Jersey City and then moved south to Baltimore and Washington. In Baltimore we played at the Royal Theater on Pennsylvania Avenue. Someone from the audience threw a bottle onstage that just missed Diana Ross. That was a rough theater. Once I was playing there when some guy shot and killed another guy over a craps game in the balcony.

As usual, when we came to Baltimore, I stayed at a family-owned boardinghouse on Dolphin Street, not too far from the Royal Theater. I went there to practice. Not long afterwards, one of the other musicians arrived at the theater.

"Joe! Don't you stay at a place on Dolphin Street?"

"Yeah, 408."

"Well, don't take my word for it, but I think there's a fire in that building."

"Damn how they look. With some grooming and the right material they're going to be good. They are going to need a lot of work, though."

"You guys sound pretty good. Maybe I can do something with it. But, what do you want to do? Do you want to record?" I said.

"Yeah. We had one company that said they would record us and told us to come over to Bobby Robinson's record session. We were at the session until three or four in the morning and then they told us to go and we didn't record."

"Well, I can't speak for anyone else, but if you want to record, I'll record you. Just to let you know how serious I am, here's a recording contract. You take it and let anybody you want to read it, your family or whoever, and then you decide." They agreed to take the contract and look it over and get back in touch with me.

I wrote down all of their names. George Smith, or "Smitty" as he was better known, was the lead vocalist. Edward "Sonny" Bivins was the first tenor and wrote songs for the group. Kenneth Kelly sang second tenor, Richard Taylor sang baritone, and Winfred "Blue" Lovett was the bass and occasional lead vocalist. They wanted to use Kenny Kelly's house as the contact address and meeting place. A day or two later, they were ready to sign with Carnival Records.

In my bones I felt this was one of the best moves I had made up to this point. Paul was less than enthusiastic but deferred to my judgment. Carnival's newest group was about to emerge.

chapter eleven

The Rise of Carnival Records

Before I went back to Motown, I met with the Manhattans at Kenny Kelly's house to rehearse. His mother owned the building. I picked some songs I wanted them to rehearse, and I rewrote several of the songs they had written. "When you get them the way I want them, then we'll record," I told the group. I always taped our rehearsals and studied the recordings very carefully. While I was in Detroit I asked Paul Williams to rehearse the group for me. I came back to New Jersey at least twice to check on their progress.

After the second trip, I told them we were ready for the studio. Paul assembled the musicians for the recording session and booked the studio time to coincide with my being in town. I had decided on recording "For the Very First Time," which Smitty wrote, and "I've Got Everything but You," one of mine. I also decided to record the track with the band and then bring in the group to record over the track, like Motown did. I brought Smitty, the lead vocalist, in to rehearse with the band, which gave the musicians some sense of how the song was supposed to sound with the singer, and a chance to test the tempo. I occasionally brought in the rest of the group to hear these sessions as well.

When I started out I was recording on four-track tapes. Track one was for the lead singer, two was for the background singers, three was for the rhythm section, and the fourth track was for whatever additional instruments were necessary. At the time, the four tracks gave me a certain amount of control over every aspect of the recording. Once that was accomplished, I had to mix it. Today, it is common to have as many as twenty-four tracks, if not more.

After completing the recording, I went back to Detroit to talk to Berry Gordy about making the Manhattans affiliate artists of Motown. I would be their manager and producer. Berry referred me to Mickey Stevenson, who was the A&R director for the label. Berry didn't want to go over Mickey's head but was definitely interested. Mickey was also interested in signing the Manhattans as Motown artists, but he wanted to handle the managing and producing internally, which would have left me with a relatively small role. After that experience with Leonard Chess, I knew I had already decided I wouldn't go for that arrangement. I was with Motown only a few months longer.

I felt it was time to devote my energy to developing Carnival Records. But first I had to resolve some personal issues. Although Taudry and I had been apart so long and hadn't seen each other in over ten years, we had not formally divorced. That action went through without complications and, after being together for close to six years, Anna and I got married in February 1963. She has been my life- and business partner ever since. She came to work part time at Carnival, which freed me up to do promotion work and set up the recording sessions. Anna took over the company's bookkeeping because Edna Johnson was too far away in the Bronx. I also hired a part-time accountant. Anna's sister, Louise, came on to help with everything else, from contacting the pressing plant and distributors to driving and working the desks.

Paul Williams's interests were actually more in the direction of booking and managing musicians than in recording them. Since we were such good friends, he decided to withdraw from the company and I reregistered Carnival Records in New Jersey at my home address, which at the time was 350 Chadwick Avenue in Newark. We never dissolved Brightstar Publishing Company, but I started a new company, Sanavan, which was a combination of the names Evans and Anna.

* * * * *

At first, the Manhattans didn't make too much noise. The second re-cording, "There Goes a Fool" and "Call Somebody Please," did a little bet-ter. I played in the band for that session. You can hear me on the flute in "There Goes a Fool." I also had the group singing live in a few places for promotional purposes. For example, there was an "Evening with the Man-hattans" program that I arranged at a local club in downtown Newark.

The test markets for recordings on the East Coast were Washington and Philadelphia. They were typical of any black record-buying market around the country. However, my test markets were Washington, Pitts-burgh, and Baltimore. Those places I knew my records would be played. It was Baltimore, however, that had the reputation for breaking new records and had become a big market, especially for introducing new artists and labels. My contacts there were extensive, going back to the days when Cee Jay Records was active. Because Jack Rags had family there, he introduced me around to all the major disc jockeys, like Al Jefferson, Kelson Fisher, Larry Dean, Sir Johnny "O", Hot Rod, Fat Daddy, and a few others. Most of them were on WWIN, one of Baltimore's most popular black stations. It was customary for the disc jockeys to have a musical theme and a radio title. For example, Al Jefferson, who was over six feet tall, was known as Al "Big Boy" Jefferson. There was also Kelson "Chop Chop" Fisher and Larry Dean, "the skinniest man you've ever seen." He wasn't that skinny, though.

Like other stations, WWIN produced a weekly chart of the top forty tunes of the week. The charting system, which was billed as "Baltimore's Authentic Music Survey," was based on record sales. Every Friday the sta-tion called local stores to find out which were the best-selling records and produced a list accordingly. There was room for abuse, manipulation, and exaggeration as there was with anything, but these were the practices of the period. I'm not even sure how they are done now.

Al Jefferson played my records all the time. We had been friends since the Cee Jay days. I would send a record to his house. If he liked it, he'd play it. If he didn't like it, he'd tell you why. He had a real talent for predicting hits. Al invited the Manhattans to Baltimore to perform at a hop, which was a dance for teenagers mostly. Those dances could literally attract more than a thousand kids. He charged admission and that's how he got paid. It was beneficial for the musicians involved because it was a promotional device for individual groups and artists, so their managements were will-ing to send them out at much lower than usual fees. Sometimes, managements would let them perform for free just to expose the group and increase record sales. This particular hop was at the Crystal Ballroom on North Avenue. Al had spun "There Goes a Fool" over the airwaves, but when he announced the Manhattans on the stage, the kids went wild. You would have thought they were the Beatles or something. They had to be held back from touching the group members. I was talking to Al about this reaction.

"They like the group well enough, but why don't they buy the record?"

"Well, I'll tell you something. Maybe the record is too pop-sounding. You know, we play it on the radio and we do get some requests, but I think it might do better on one of the white pop stations. You might need their help to break it. It almost sounds like the Four Seasons. But the kids are excited about the group."

After the concert I told Blue Lovett, "Well, they like the group and while you're fresh on their minds we're going to produce another recording that's a little more in the groove. I'm going to let 'There Goes a Fool' and 'Call Somebody Please' run their course, but when they take it off the air, we'll be ready with another record." That's when we recorded "I Wanna Be."

"I Wanna Be (Your Everything)" was a song Blue had written earlier, but, as the bass vocalist in the group, he was singing it in his lower range. When I met the Manhattans for their rehearsal at Kenny Kelly's house, we were going through possible songs to record. When we got to "I Wanna Be," I decided that was the song we'd do. I wanted to alter the range, though. I wanted it sung higher than Blue had been doing it and I wanted Blue to sing the lead. Blue was hesitant to do so because he wasn't comfortable singing in that range.

"If you want it there, let Smitty sing the lead," he said.

"No. I want you to sing in the top of your voice so we can get more tension." That's what I was looking for. I wanted the vocal tension that communicated a sense of urgency, reaching, and excitement. So he sang it in one key, but I raised it a couple of keys so he'd have to reach. It wasn't too comfortable, but he did a nice job. Blue kept trying to insist, "Let Smitty sing it. Let Smitty sing it." "No, I want you to do it," I said. So that's the way we rehearsed it.

The recording session took place at Talent Masters Studio down on Forty-second Street in Manhattan. Bob Gallo was the recordist and engineer. I was working on the mixing. Someone let a lady in the studio during the mixing and pointed me out to her. She looked at me and said, "This one?" Someone from the front said, "Yeah." She came over.

"Mister, can I buy that record? Who's the group singing?" she asked. I thought Bob was playing a joke, which I was in no mood for.

"Lady, I'm busy. Please don't do this. I can't be bothered," I told her.

"No, I'm not kidding. I'm up in the beauty shop over the studio. The ladies up there sent me down to find out whose record it was and who the group is because they want to buy it," she said.

"Oh, yeah?" I looked at Bob and he said, "I didn't do it. I thought it was a good sign, so I just sent her to you."

"Okay, you can buy it next week. The name of the song is 'I Wanna Be' by the Manhattans," I told her politely. She got a pencil and wrote it down.

"Can I get it any sooner than next week?" she asked.

"No, we have to put the finishing touches on the recording and it won't be ready until then." I agreed with Bob that it was a good sign.

Al Jefferson had agreed to spin "There Goes a Fool" and "Call Somebody Please" on WWIN a little longer. I made seven dubs of "I Wanna Be" and started out for Baltimore. I made it to WWIN just as Kelson Fisher went on the air. The station was upstairs over a bank. Kelson was a smooth cat who was rarely disturbed by anything, and he loved Old Grand Dad whiskey. After I got to the station, Kelson and I talked a while. I asked him, "Do you want a taste?"—which meant whiskey—and he said, "Sure. You know what I drink." He was a dyed-in-the-wool Old Grand Dad drinker. I went across the street and stocked up on it and a case of beer.

"What you got, Joe?"

"This is the newest Manhattan record." He listened to it over his earphones and said he liked it. "Let's get on it," he said. Kelson started to play "I Wanna Be" shortly after his 7 P.M. show began. He had a real smooth speaking voice, especially over the radio. Kelson was spinning the records and drinking the Old Grand Dad. I was in the control room with him as the switchboard for incoming calls lit up. He was talking to callers and I thought I heard him refer to the Manhattans but I wasn't really paying close attention. After several calls, he casually turned to me and said, "Joe, I think you got something here. You know who all these calls were for? They were calling about your record."

"Are you kidding?" I thought he was jiving me.

"No. I'm not kidding." The next call that came, he put it on intercom so I could answer it. Sure enough, it was a request for "I Wanna Be." Kelson got a few more calls, but after drinking the whiskey he was high as hell. He decided to let me answer the next call.

The phone rang and I answered, "WWIN, the Kelson Fisher Show." This man asked in a very coarse voice, "Who's this?"

"Joe Evans, promotion man for Carnival Records."

"Well, look here, Joe. Who them niggas singing 'I Need to Be' . . . 'You Gonna Be' . . . 'I Ought to Be' . . . 'What's It Gonna Be?'" Just then I heard a voice from the background call out, "I Want to Be . . ." "Oh, 'I Wanna Be.' Who is that by?"

I said, "It's by a new group called the Manhattans."

"Well, are you one of 'em?" he said.

"No. I'm a promotion man for Carnival Records."

He said, "Man, I gotta get that record. Can I buy it?"

"Sure. Just go down to your record shop," I said. I just told him that to generate interest.

He said, "Look here, I'm layin' up here right now with my woman. She's telling me I gotta get that damn record for her. So, man, she will kill me if I don't get it. What's those guys' name?"

"The Manhattans."

"Spell it."

"M-A-N-H-A-T-T-A-N-S."

"Yeah, I got it. And who did it?"

"Carnival Records."

"Okay, Joe. Thanks."

When he hung up, another line lit up. The next call was from some young girls and they were asking, "Mister, who is singing that record, 'I Oughta Be' or something or 'Gotta Be' something?" So I had to tell them who it was and they were just giggling. These sounded like preteen girls and they were just laughing on the telephone, asking me questions like, "Are they nice-looking boys?"

"Yeah, I guess they look all right," I said.

"Yeah. How many of them is it?"

"Five."

"Well, there ought to be one in there for me."

I just smiled and shook my head. By that time Kelson had downed whiskey and beer, but you could never tell it in his speaking voice. His shift ended at 1 A.M.

He left damn near drunk and the next DJ, John Compton or "Sir Johnny 'O,'" came on for the rest of the night. I knew him real well, too.

After he played the song and listened to it through his headphones, he said, "Yeah, that sounds nice, Joe. I think you got a good one here." Sir Johnny "O" was fun because he loved to play those records. He was younger than the rest of the other disc jockeys. He had a smooth line of talk and used more flash than Kelson or Al Jefferson, but he carried the

1 A.M. to 6 A.M. shift, which was rough. He didn't get the opportunity to meet many of the promotion men because he came on so late in the night. He was pleased to have me there for a change. I stayed the whole night. We left the station at 6 and met up with some other disc jockeys and went to breakfast. I was so tired I didn't finish my breakfast. I barely made it to the Sheraton Hotel right up the street and passed out.

About ten or eleven in the morning, the phone in my room rang. Before I could even say hello, I heard "Hey, Joe!"

"Who is this?"

"Chick Silvers."

"How did you know I was here?"

"I saw Johnny 'O' and some guys from the radio station and they told me where to find you." Chick Silvers was the promotion man for Musical Sales, my record distributor.

"Look, I'm calling about your record," he said.

"What record?" I was still in a daze.

"The one they played last night on the radio. Some record shops have already come in asking about it. We even got a show committee asking about it."

I told him, "I don't have the record. They were playing dubs."

"You don't have the record? Man, look here. You gonna let us have it when it comes out?"

"Yeah, you can distribute it, but you have to sell more records than you did the last two times."

"Yeah, man, don't worry. It's starting off good. I swear you're getting calls. When are you going back to Jersey?" Chick was in a hurry.

"Today. Right after I get some sleep."

"When you get back I want you to send me 1,300 as soon as you can get them here."

"You're not gonna let them sit back there on the floor, are you?" I asked.

"With the initial reaction, I'm going to sell that many easily," he said.

I made it back to Jersey to put in my order for 1,000 copies, or "pieces," as we called them, of the record but only sent Chick Silver 650 copies. They weren't that expensive, around a dime a record. The copies from the stampers came relatively fast and I shipped them by Greyhound to Baltimore. Two days later, Chick called me at Carnival's office.

"Joe, I got the 650 you sent, but we are back-ordered 650 and I need another 1,300."

"What are you doing with the records I sent?" I asked.

"Those went and I haven't supplied all my people. So I gave those you sent to my best customers, but everyone has to have them."

"All right," I said. I sent another 650 and Chick called back.

"Joe, I received the shipment of 650 so I am now back-ordered 1,300. I want to place another order of 1,300 records on top of that." I became a little suspicious and decided to go down to Baltimore and see what the demand was like for myself.

I caught the Greyhound. I got off the bus and walked up and down Pennsylvania Avenue, a major black section of town on the west side. Past the Royal Theater, which I had played and knew well, I went in record shop after record shop and asked, "Do you have the record 'I Wanna Be' by the Manhattans?" The routine answer was they had run out of copies. One guy said, "Yeah. Yeah." He went back to check and came back and said, "Sorry, I don't have anymore. I only got a few of them to begin with. Come back tomorrow. I'll get it for you. It seems like some chicken-shit little record company's got it and they won't give me but so many. People have been calling for it." Another store had just sold their last copy. I said to myself, "There *is* a demand for it."

I went home and had some more pieces pressed, but I knew I wouldn't be able to keep up with the kind of demand "I Wanna Be" was generating. I checked back with the distributor for Baltimore, Washington, and Virginia. They only gave me around $1,200 as an advance. To break out of the Baltimore/Washington market, I needed more money to do some serious production.

First, I went to a New York distributor called Portum Records. There was a lady there named Miss Pare. Initially, she wasn't impressed, but I put on my best sales pitch and she came around and gave me a small advance, which went directly into more pressings. I then went to the black station WLIB in New York to see the disc jockey Tommy Smalls, whose radio name was "Dr. Jive." Tommy and I had known each other for some time from the NATRA conventions, Tangerine, and Cee Jay.

"Look, Tommy, I got this record. I don't have no money right now, but if you help me, I'll take care of you when I get some."

Tommy said, "Aw, Joe, I'd play it for you for nothing, but I'm afraid you're going to lose your record. One of those big companies is going to cover if you can't supply it. They'll take it away from you. You might want to take it to a bigger company before it's stolen."

"Yeah? Let 'em cover it. They'll still have to pay me the publishing rights," I said. Inside I had a feeling no one could cover the song the way

I recorded it, but I didn't say so. "You play it for me and I'll take care of you."

Tommy said, "All right. Look, here's what you do. Take it to this company and make a deal with them. They'll take the record over and get it around for you. You tell them I sent you."

It was a small label, though. Tommy said, "When they get straight with you, I'll play it." He wrote the company name down on a piece of paper and I left. But I wasn't going where he sent me, because I was suspicious. I had, after all, had that Gladys Knight incident a few years earlier fresh on my mind. "I Wanna Be" had to stay on Carnival Records.

I was on the subway when I remembered this white New York disc jockey whom I had met when I was with Motown, Murray the K. He had said he would help me when I got my company started by playing my records if they were good. Murray the K was with WINS, one of the biggest stations in the city, with a large audience, and he was one of the two big names in the New York market. I went to the upstairs area of the building where WINS broadcast from and asked a receptionist if I could see Murray the K. She directed me where to go and I made it to the door of his office on the second floor. A man was guarding the door who wouldn't let me in to see Murray. He looked like he could have been a gangster. I explained, "I have a record. I met Murray when I was with Motown and he said he'd help me when my record came out. I wanted to talk to him and give him the record."

This tough guy said, "Well, I'll see that he gets it."

I wrote Murray a brief note to recall our meeting and his offer to help me to promote my record and gave it to the tough guy and started back toward the elevator. Just then, Murray stuck his head out the door.

"Joe! Joe!!"

"Yeah!" I ran back down the hall.

"Murray, this is the group I was telling you about and I'm getting some action on it down in Baltimore and Washington. It's real nice action, man, and it's happening. Man, just take a listen to it. You take a listen to it and let me know."

"All right. I'll tell you what I'm going to do. I'm going to put it on my show tonight," he said. He had a show where he played new records and listeners called in to determine a winner, second, and third place. So he said, "Let's see if it makes a good showing. People will call in and vote for the record. If it comes up tonight and does good, I'll put it on tomorrow night. If it does all right in there, I'll get it on the program list."

"Yeah? You'd do this for me? Look here, I don't have no money, but man, you know, you help me with it, I'll remember it and I'll appreciate it."

"Man, I can't ask you for any money. How can you give money for something? You haven't sold nothing yet," he said.

I went back to New Jersey feeling just fine. I told the Manhattans that "I Wanna Be" was to be aired that night on the Murray the K show in New York, which they didn't believe. They were excited when they heard themselves over the airwaves that evening. The first night the song ended up in third place, but by the third night it was in the number one spot. What was more amazing is that WMCA, New York City's largest station, which also had a predominantly white audience, started playing it the following week. Jack Lacey was the daytime disc jockey for WINS and he was giving the song play during the day. Before the week was out, it was in the number ten position on that station and had successfully crossed over from the black listeners to the general public. That had the effect of helping the song to break in other large markets like Boston, Chicago, Cleveland, Detroit, and Pittsburgh. I went back to Miss Pare at Portum Records and she authorized further cash advances based on listener response.

Sometime after all this activity I got a call one evening from Tommy Smalls.

"Uh . . . hi Joe! How ya doin'?"

"Pretty good, Tommy."

"You know I'm playing your record, don't you?"

"Well, I don't listen to your station that much, but I guess if you say you're playing it, you're playing it."

"You're getting calls on it, aren't you? Then you know I must be on it."

I was thinking to myself, "What does this son of a bitch want?" He was trying to take credit for the success of "I Wanna Be" breaking big in New York. He had no idea I had gone to Murray the K and *begged* him to play my record. It was Murray who opened the way for me. You had to be a genius working with disc jockeys, or a top psychologist. Some of those players were planning how to prey on you when you were asleep. They were always hustling, you know. Not always trying to get money, but advantages.

Tommy rambled on some more, but finally came to the point of the call. "You know since I helped you out with your record, I got a show planned for the Apollo. You gotta give me a deal on booking the Manhattans. Don't charge me the full amount."

"Look, the Manhattans are signed with Shaw Artists now," which was the booking agent I used for the group. "You go down there and talk to them. I don't have anything to do with that."

"Well, you know, you're over the group. You can tell 'em what to do," he said.

"Well, I'll put in a good word for you because I appreciate what you're doing." He actually didn't do a thing but jump on the bandwagon.

When I got a call from a London distributor asking me if they could handle it in Europe, I knew I would need more money, substantial money, to deal with my supply problem. Every time I put in an order for pressing, I had to go over and pay in cash.

I went to Columbia Products, the division that did the pressing for Columbia Records, to ask for help. I spoke to a Mr. Grant and I was ready to do my "poor-mouth" routine once more. I told him how I had difficulty in getting credit through the banks to get additional record pressings done. He said, "Let me see the receipts from your previous sales and pressings." I produced those and he studied them carefully. Then he said, "You shouldn't be having trouble getting credit at the bank because you are current with all your bills and your paid receipts should have established your credit. I can see you know what you're doing. As soon as you get the money, you don't fiddle around with it. So you want us to press the record for you?"

"Yeah."

"You go and have the parts made up and sent to us and we'll make them. When you're ready to put in an order, just call my girl."

Columbia had major facilities and could press records in large volume. Twenty-five thousand was my average on the Manhattans. They had pressing plants that distributed around the entire country. My supply problems were finally gone. "I Wanna Be" broke onto the national charts by February 1965 and continued to climb. It eventually made its way to number twelve on the national rhythm and blues chart and to number sixty-eight on the national crossover pop chart. The record sold over half a million copies and was the Manhattans' biggest hit prior to their signing with Columbia Records in the 1970s.

With the reputation of the Manhattans and Carnival Records firmly established, the work, in many ways, had just begun. I had to create an image for the group. I started by taking them to Shaw Artists, who began to book them on shows. When Shaw didn't have a booking, I scheduled them. I didn't treat them like artists. They were more like my sons. I paid rents on occasion and bought suits for them to perform in. Two sets meant ten suits and they were tailor-made for each of them. They were routinely mentioned in *Billboard* magazine and were on its cover at least once.

The Manhattans' follow-up recording was "Searchin' for My Baby" and "I'm the One That Love Forgot." This was a two-sided hit. "I'm the One That Love Forgot" was particularly well received in Philadelphia and Pittsburgh. This reception was made possible through the help of disc jockey Jocko Henderson. Jocko was well known in the New York area but had an even greater following and influence in the Philadelphia area. He had an affinity for rhythm and blues. He really pushed "I'm the One That Love Forgot," even though it was on side B. Jocko then booked the group to appear at a theater in Brooklyn and the headline singer was Otis Redding.

Part of the grooming process for the Manhattans involved my standing backstage and giving them directions, which might include miming stylized gestures with my hands, which they imitated; how and when to acknowledge applause; and general stage presence. I was standing in the wings directing the group from backstage when I was approached by Otis Redding.

"That's your group?" he asked. I nodded yes but was still paying attention to what the group was doing onstage. "They are fantastic, especially the lead singer! I'm getting ready to do a tour of several black colleges and I'd like to take your group with me." I lit up then and was paying full attention to *him*.

"All right, I'll okay it with Shaw." Otis Redding's manager called me with the dates and the details. They would be the opening act and Otis's management would supply the accommodations and transportation. This would be the group's first road tour. They toured mostly in the South, where the majority of black colleges were, but also played as far north as Wilberforce in Ohio. The tour lasted a little more than a month.

Near the end of 1965, Carnival posted another hit with the Manhattans, "Follow Your Heart." It was paired with "The Boston Monkey," which didn't do quite as well. "Follow Your Heart" also sold over half a million copies and reached *Billboard*'s rhythm and blues chart as well as several pop charts. Other acts and groups were beginning to be referred to me for possible affiliation with Carnival. Blue referred several, including Curby Goggins, who recorded "Come Home to Daddy" and "Love Me if You Want To." Norma Jenkins, Phil Terrell, and the Lovettes were also Blue referrals. I believe Phil was related to Blue. He had been going to school at Elizabeth City State in North Carolina. His recordings did okay, but none of them were big hits. Other groups like the Pets and Leon and the Metronomes were produced by someone else, but their records were released on Carnival. Others in that category were Little Royal, Jimmy Jules, and Harold and Connie. Maurice Simon and the Pie Men were produced by Dick Vance and released on Carnival.

Some groups were "Hollywood"-type discoveries, like Lee Williams and the Cymbals. One Sunday I was walking down 128th Street somewhere near

Seventh Avenue and passed by a brownstone house and heard this singing. I stopped and listened to it a while. I knocked at a nearby door and asked a lady where the sound was coming from. She directed me to a basement area, which wasn't easy to get to. These boys were out in the backyard of the building. One of them came up and I told him I was a record producer and he invited me over to where they were rehearsing. They continued to sing and I was especially impressed with the lead and how well the group blended.

"Who do you all record for?" I asked.

"We don't record for anybody. We're just rehearsing," Lee said. I gave them one of my cards and told them to give me a call. They called me back immediately. They came and sang some things I didn't like. I had this boy Ronnie McCoy, who later became a member of the Topics, who was routinely writing songs and sending them to me. He had written a song, "I Love You More," which was pretty good. He wanted to record it himself and kept after me, but I thought Lee's voice was better suited for it. I asked Ronnie to sing it on a tape and gave it to Lee Williams to learn. In about two weeks the group was ready for the studio. "I Love You More" was a big hit in several markets. It did real well in Chicago and Philadelphia. That success was followed by an appearance by Lee Williams and the Cymbals in Chicago's Regal Theater.

The Manhattans' recordings, in the meantime, were still gaining momentum. Other well-received singles were "Can I," which was cowritten by Smitty and me; "I Bet'cha (Couldn't Love Me)"; and "It's That Time of the Year" and "Alone on New Year's Eve," which was a well-received Christmas release. The Lovettes were the backup female group on those releases. As the strongest recording group of Carnival Records, the Manhattans deserved special attention, which they received. I bought a van with the Manhattans advertised on the side of the vehicle for them to tour in. They also began attracting attention from rival companies and labels. I had them at the Apollo and noticed these guys hanging around the boys in the group. They might not have attracted my attention had I not seen these same guys with the Manhattans earlier that same day. It turned out they were record producers from other companies trying to butter them up to switch labels. Those rival producers had no idea I was paying rent, providing transportation, buying uniforms, and the whole bit. I even had to get a few of them out of run-ins with the law.

Smitty was a talented singer but didn't manage his personal life nearly as well as he sang. The Manhattans had a date in Newark and were scheduled to leave immediately for Atlanta for a performance. I got a call from a detective friend of mine who told me an arrest warrant was about to be issued for Smitty. His estranged wife was seeking back alimony payments. I had this sinking feeling about the whole situation. When I caught up with Smitty I told him, "Take the night off. Let Blue do the singing. What you do is come in later in the evening and see how the lay of the land is. Do a number or two and scoot out of there. Don't show up with Blue or the rest of them, so they'll think you aren't showing and whoever is around there waiting for you will go away." "All right," he said, but instead went right up there with the other boys and started singing. I was home in bed and got a call from another detective who was at the place where the Manhattans were singing.

"Joe, I got this boy, the lead singer, Smitty. He's wanted for alimony and I'm going to have to lock him up."

I jumped up and said, "Please, don't do that! There are people there who've paid money to hear the group. Look, I'm on my way. I'll take care of things when I get there. Then you can take him."

"Okay, I won't bother him until they're finished," he told me. When they finished, Smitty was arrested and taken to jail there in Newark.

I went to the Jersey City precinct where I knew people and asked the captain to look out for him. The captain told me he wasn't there, but in Newark. He said, "He probably won't be here until Monday morning if they bring him then. It could be as late as Wednesday."

"What? That boy's got to be in Atlanta, Georgia, on Monday!" The captain said they had to make arrangements to go over there and get him. I pleaded, "Please, I'll take care of you, but I gotta get that boy. It'll kill him if he misses that performance in Atlanta."

Just then two patrolmen came in dressed in riot gear. The captain told them to go to Newark and get Smitty. They were as mad as hell. It was about three in the morning. I sat at the police station the rest of the night. It was six in the morning when they got back. When Smitty first saw me he smiled, and then he started crying. I said, "You know, you didn't listen to me and do like I told you. And as a result, here you are."

He just hung his head down, still sobbing, "I know. I know." They took him in the back and locked him up. I went to the captain again and he gave me the name of a reliable bailbondsman. I called him and explained the situation to him and told him about the urgency regarding Smitty's being in Atlanta for a performance on Monday. The bailbondsman told me he'd get Smitty out. Later that Sunday morning he got him freed. I told the bailbondsman I would straighten things out with him when he got back in town, but I arranged for Louise to go to the airport to pay him, since Smitty was about to fly out of town. Smitty made the performance.

Before he could leave town, though, there was a hearing, which I attended on his behalf. I spoke to the judge, who asked if I, as Smitty's manager, would be responsible for collecting the alimony payments so the girl wouldn't have to chase him down again. I said, "Judge, I make the contracts, but I don't keep up with them like that. The best I can do is to remind him, but I can't punish him and take his money." When we got outside of the courtroom, I told Smitty, "All right, remember before you start drinking, you get that money in the mail, so they don't pick you up again when you come into town."

* * * * *

Carnival Records was growing steadily. Anna and Louise were still working there, even though when we started we were working off the kitchen table. When Paul and I started I had about five hundred dollars. After the break of "I Wanna Be" and subsequent successes, the company was consistently selling more than half a million records. By today's standards that may not be large, but it was considerable for a small label of that period. My overall plan was to build the Manhattans into a powerhouse group and then bring in other affiliate artists. I wanted to duplicate on the East Coast what Berry Gordy had done in Detroit, that is, create a black-owned recording company with a solid reputation for excellence. The bigger we got, the more pressure was brought on us.

Larger record companies started calling about specific records with requests to sell them on their label and give me a percentage of the sales. I heard from Atlantic, Kapp, ABC, Paramount, and several others. I generally strung them along with the standard phrase, "Let me get back to you." I also had offers to sell the company. Other companies got the idea that we had something and wanted to buy it. But they also wanted to control it. They wanted more percentage than I was ready to offer. For example, one company wanted a 60 percent controlling interest and offered to make me a vice president in the company. They took me to lunch with the directors and the whole bit. When I came back, I didn't do anything about it. At the same time companies were sending out runners to see if they could lure Carnival artists away with promises of a better and more lucrative situation if they signed with them. After Lee Williams and the Cymbals, the Topics joined the label. They were another moneymaking group.

When Carnival started to produce albums, we did even better. *Dedicated to You* was our first Manhattans album and *For You and Yours* was the second. The albums increased our revenues considerably. Along with the Manhattans, Lee Williams and the Cymbals were the biggest moneymakers for the label.

We eventually moved the company from 350 Chadwick Avenue downtown to a proper office space, 24 Branford Place in Newark. Before we did so, however, there was an amusing incident that took place at the Chadwick address. Louise was working the desk and looked out the window and noticed a white man walking around our house and looking down at some notes. We had a vacant lot next to our house, so I thought he was looking at that property, but he was in our yard. I decided to go out and see what he wanted.

"Can I help you?" I asked.

"Yeah. I'm looking for Carnival Record Company. Could you tell me where that is?"

"Yes. This is it."

He looked at me as if puzzled. "Well, I'm looking for Carnival Records. Where would that be?"

"Right in this house," I said.

He identified himself as a representative of Dunn and Bradstreet, the Wall Street investment company. I invited him inside.

"I was given this assignment to look into. Someone applied for credit," he said.

"That was me. I'm Joe Evans, the president of Carnival Records."

"Do you have accounts receivable and all other relevant information available for me to examine?"

"Sure."

"And your books?" Anna got the books and other material out, but before I let him look at anything I made him show me his identification verifying that he indeed worked for Dunn and Bradstreet. He could have been a spy from a rival company trying to determine just how solvent my company was or how vulnerable it was to a takeover or buyout. Such tactics were not unheard of.

He looked at the books and came back to me.

"Where is the inventory?" I told him we didn't keep the inventory at the Chadwick address. "Well, how do you get to do all this business? What are you selling?" he asked as he looked around.

I told him records, which he was trying to locate. "We don't keep records here. The records are pressed and they are put into a warehouse store over at another location. As we get the orders from the distributors, the pressers produce the records and ship them around the country and to overseas distributors. We send the bill to the distributor after the shipment. Every order has a number and it is reflected in the book that way."

The man seemed a little suspicious somehow. He asked, "How did you learn to do that? Where did you get the idea? From what country?"

"Well, I just learned it from paying attention to what other small companies were doing."

"How many people do you have working for you?" he asked.

"Here we are. Anna, my wife; Louise, my sister-in-law; and me. Of course, we have people helping us with promotional activities."

"How about your warehouse? You have to pay to store records there, don't you?"

"No," I told him. "We press enough to cover orders and just ship them."

He asked a few more detailed questions and then left. He must have given us a very favorable report because we did receive a triple A rating. The Dunn and Bradstreet rating helped us to incorporate the business and the publishing company. It also meant that more companies were calling about a merger or a buyout. Things were clicking right along.

· · · · ·

It was 1969 and Carnival Records was still enjoying relative success. The Manhattans' reputation was solid and they had two more years on their contract with me. They were still being approached by other producers, but that had been a reality for some years by that time. The first hint I got that trouble was brewing was when the Manhattans were grumbling about showing up at rehearsals and not following my directions. In hindsight there were other behavioral signs that indicated what lay ahead. Finally, Blue, as the spokesman, started saying things like, other people said they should be in Hollywood or with a much bigger label. At least that was the view according to some other producers. That was followed by their general dissatisfaction with the way things were going. I told them, "Look at your figures and you'll see that each year you've done 50 percent better than the year before and that's a good record. You know where you came from. We started at ground zero." After some stalling and my trying to persuade the group that things weren't as bad as they thought, they made it clear they wanted to leave Carnival. I was determined to put my personal feelings aside at the time and do my best to handle this as a business situation.

I wanted to place them with a bigger label that had a larger budget for promotion and other trappings. This meant selling their contract. I spoke to several companies. United Artists was the biggest. I knew a vice president there, Ed Wright, who used to be a disc jockey in Cleveland and then went to United Artists to run their record division.

"I'll take them today, but are you going to produce them?" he asked.

I said, "Naw, I'm just selling the group. They want to split and I want to satisfy 'em."

I talked to a few other companies like Kapp and Jubilee, and all of them were willing to take them, but all of them wanted me to continue to produce them. I then contacted Atlantic Records, but I did so through my attorney, Warren Troob. He came back and said the same thing. Then I spoke to a representative who told me, "Joe, it would be better for you to produce them because you know their temperament and style."

I said, "They want to leave and I don't think they want me to produce them anymore."

The representative shot back, "If we're buying their contract, we tell *them* who'll be producing them."

"Okay," I said.

"Just help get us up off the ground with them and we'll take it from there," he said.

I reluctantly agreed, but in all honesty my heart wasn't in it. Those feelings between me and the group had been lost, so for me it would be a business arrangement.

Atlantic would have been a good company for the Manhattans. That was the hottest rhythm and blues label at the time and I figured it would be able to move the Manhattans forward professionally. I asked Warren to draw up a contract. Atlantic required all our signatures. I signed and all he needed was the group's signature to seal the deal with Atlantic. Warren came back with the contract unsigned and told me the group had hired their own lawyer, Jack Pearl, who told them not to sign the contract with Atlantic. I then went to them and asked for an explanation. One of them, I don't remember who, said, "Our lawyer told us don't sign no contract with Atlantic."

"What do you mean? Atlantic is one of the hottest labels around. They've got good hours and you know what they pay. They're gonna go all out for you." I then told them, "All right. What about United Artist or Kapp?"

They kept heehawing and that's when I picked up that something was happening. They had been instructed by their lawyer. I went back to Warren, who was able to find out that Jack Pearl "threw a monkey wrench in the deal." He also found out that Jack Pearl was trying to sell the group to the Deluxe label, which was no larger than Carnival and had all but gone inactive. Deluxe had done some good things in the past but hadn't produced anything of late. Warren surmised they were trying to use the Manhattans to reactivate Deluxe Records. Something was definitely wrong. Deluxe wasn't as large as Carnival, and the group supposedly wanted a bigger label. It was later that I learned that Jack Pearl had relatives who had a financial interest in Deluxe.

Apparently the decision to reject the Atlantic offer and sign with Deluxe was not unanimous within the group. Sonny Bivins came to me and told me he intended to quit the Manhattans. I told him to stay. I said, "You have to look out for yourself. Just remember. A lawyer is supposed to carry out the ideas *you* want carried out. He's not your boss. You tell him what you want and he's supposed to make it happen for you."

The more I thought about the Manhattans' rejecting the Atlantic deal, the more disgusted I became. I put so much of my life into building the Manhattan phenomena. I called Warren Troob and told him to sell the contract. I didn't care if he stood on a corner and gave it away for thirty dollars. I just didn't care. Troob laughed and said, "Let's see if we can salvage something more than that." He went back to Jack Pearl and came up with an agreement for the Manhattans to record one more album for Carnival with no royalties and a few thousand dollars. I wasn't thrilled with the arrangement but Troob said I would draw in more money from the sale of the album. We were supposed to record eight songs, but I only recorded three, "I Don't Want to Go," "Love Is Breaking Out (All Over)," and "'Til You Come Back to Me." After that I lost interest and didn't bother about recording anymore. I was down and just let it go at that. In hindsight, it wasn't a good decision for me to forgo the rest of that session. It took a toll on me financially as well. Before, Carnival Records was coming out with consistent hits. The Manhattans' departure caused my line of credit to be jeopardized, as well as other financial deals that I might have been able to pull off had they stayed. I was disheartened by what had happened and felt betrayed, but in the end I realized I loved those guys. You can't create something like that from nothing and completely turn your back on it.

I kept up with the Manhattans' activities somewhat after they left. About four months or so after they split, I was in New York and ran into Smitty. I happened to know the group was on tour in the Midwest.

"What are you doing here?" I asked.

"Oh, Joe, I wasn't feeling well. I'm going to join them later."

When I reflected back on that conversation, I realized he must have been too ashamed to tell me he had been put out of the group. He had been showing up "drunk" and not performing well. It turned out, however, that Smitty was suffering from the effects of a head injury he had received some time earlier. He began having fainting episodes that members of the group thought were caused by drunkenness. He never really took good care of himself. I had to put him in the hospital a few times for pneumonia when the group was with me. He'd drink wine and walk outside with his collar open and before you knew it he'd lose his voice or have laryngitis. I guess I had a greater affinity for him because I had to look out after him more than the others. Smitty was unquestionably a talented singer. But as is often the case with such talent, he was quite fragile, with several insecurities.

The irony of this was that had I known the Manhattans had put Smitty out, I could have built another group around him. After all, he was the lead and it would have been no trouble at all.

Toye Kates, the group's onetime road manager, kept me posted on much of the Manhattans' activities after their departure from Carnival. It was some time after I saw Smitty in New York when Toye told me Smitty was "in a bad way" in the hospital. He said Sonny Bivins had gone to visit him at his house and saw that he was real sick. His family must have belonged to a Holiness Sanctified or a similar praying church or something and told Bivins that Smitty had just been prayed over the night before as well as the previous week. Bivins insisted on putting him in the hospital and Toye let me know which one he was in. Toye was also supposed to let me know when the visiting hours were so I could go and see Smitty. The following day Toye called.

"Joe, it's too late. He's gone."

"Gone where?" I asked.

"He's dead."

I could hardly believe it. George Smith died on December 17, 1970, of a subdural hematoma.

Within a few years the Manhattans left the Deluxe label to sign with Columbia Records. It was with Columbia that they eventually became a million-seller group. Their climb to that level took ten years and several personnel changes, but it all started while they were Carnival artists. It was my label that made their name and reputation.

After losing the Manhattans I wondered if I should lease the company or just sell it outright. I thought maybe I should reconsider some of the earlier offers to merge with another company. In the end, I decided that Carnival Records should remain with me.

I'm sure that at some level owning Carnival filled a gap in my own family experience. My attempting to replace or at least neutralize it explained what happened in my relationship with the Manhattans. Those guys were like my sons. I wondered at the time if the way the group left me was a form of punishment for having not stayed in contact with my family in Pensacola.

I think if I could have stayed in closer contact with Smitty, I might have been able to save his life. But there was little use crying over spilled milk or what I didn't do. The thing that I did, for good or bad, was to go and get another glass.

Joe Evans in Jerusalem with
the Lionel Hampton band, 1954.

Joe Evans at Café Society, New York City, 1954.

On the boat returning from Italy, 1954.

Joe Evans (left)
with Johnny Hodges,
c. 1958.

The Manhattans, 1962.

The Manhattans, 1963.

George "Smitty" Smith, c. 1967.

Joe and Anna Evans in Richmond, Virginia, c. 1994.

Joe Evans at ninety, October 2006. Collection of Christopher Brooks.

chapter twelve

After the Manhattans

I was sitting in my office considering options, when I heard an announcement over the radio: "You can go to college on weekends, in the evenings, even on Sundays; just come to Essex County College for more information." Essex County College was just a few blocks away from my office on Clinton Street in downtown Newark. I could take some business courses to rebuild and strengthen Carnival.

The following day, during my lunch break, I went to the registrar at Essex and started asking questions about certain courses. I thought there would be a bunch of kids in there, but instead, I saw other adults in my age range.

I thought to myself, "I might be all right here." In the section of the application about where I attended high school, I put Washington High in Pensacola, Florida. The next item was, "Year graduated."

"Damn, look here. I forgot that I didn't get my high school diploma," I said with some embarrassment to the person taking the applications.

135

Without so much as a flinch, the registrar asked, "What grade did you complete?"

"I think the eleventh and part of the twelfth."

"That's okay," he said. "You can get a GED."

"GED? What's that?"

"That's a high school equivalency exam. There are two ways you can do it. You can take courses until you get enough credits to get a GED, or you can just take the test."

It was obvious to me that this young man had been through this scenario before.

"When is the test offered?" I asked.

"Every month. You just pay the fee for the exam."

"Well, sign me up for the next test."

The young man looked a little concerned. "You want to take this test without any preparation?"

"Sure," I said. Within a few days, I was back to take the test.

Even though I hadn't formally finished high school, I had been an avid reader and thought the test couldn't be too bad. It wasn't and I passed it. My counselor told me that I didn't have to take any remedial courses, but I did take the placement test. Although I had exempted out of remedial English and math, that algebra course kicked the hell out of me. The funny thing is that although I just wanted to take a business course, I was registered for everything *but* business.

After my first semester as a full-time student, I was hooked. My education became my new priority. I reconciled myself to the reality of being unable to keep Carnival Records active and be a committed full-time student, too. I decided to lease parts of the Carnival catalog and go to school. This was my new challenge. I took every course I could manage—Western civilization, philosophy, sociology, history, and whatever else was offered. There was no half-stepping. I was the classic older-than-average student. I read even more than I had before and was always willing to participate in class discussions.

There were many great instructors at Essex from whom I learned a good deal. They were always willing to help you. Among them was my old friend Aaron Bell, who had played with me in Andy Kirk's band and in my group, Joe Evans and His Bell Boys, some years earlier. He was working on a doctorate at Columbia at the time and was teaching in the music department at Essex. After receiving his Ph.D., he became the chair of the department.

The education bug infected the Evans household. Anna also started taking classes and received an associate's degree in sociology. It was the spring of 1973 and just a few months before I was supposed to graduate from Essex. I noticed an announcement on the advertisement board outside the counseling office about a Ford Foundation scholarship. I spoke to my counselor, Calvin Woodland (who was also working on a doctorate), and he thought that with my good grades I should apply for it. In fact, he did most of the legwork for me, and he even helped me fill out the application and edited the required essay for the competition. The institution had to support the candidate and do the formal nomination. I was informed a few months later that I had won one of the grants. It was a scholarship that would pay all of my school expenses (tuition, room and board, and a stipend) to any four-year college or university that accepted me. I could hardly believe it was happening.

Before too long, I started receiving letters from colleges and universities around the country, congratulating me for my receipt of the Ford Foundation scholarship and inviting me to apply to their institutions. Among the institutions that I heard from were Penn State, University of Chicago, West Virginia University, Macalester College, Bishop College, Virginia Union University, Susquehanna University, Syracuse University, University of Kentucky, University of Virginia, Aquinas College, and many others. There were more than one hundred letters of invitation. I was receiving five and six a day.

I didn't hear from Rutgers University but did arrange an interview with a counselor at the Newark campus. That's where I wanted to attend. The young man whom I spoke to looked over my record and after studying it carefully said, "I think it would be a waste of time for you to go to a four-year college. We would love to have you, but I think you should get into law school or maybe even graduate school. As much as we'd hate to lose you, I'll send you down to the main campus in New Brunswick." I wasn't thrilled with the idea of all the traveling, but this appeared to be an opportunity worth following up. The counselor said, "I'm sending you to a man named Dr. Samuel Proctor at the Rutgers New Brunswick campus."

The late Samuel Proctor was a well-known and highly respected educator. He had been president of Virginia Union University in Richmond and had also held other prestigious positions around the country. He was the director of a program at Rutgers called the Career Opportunity Program (COP), which identified gifted and talented students at the two-year (associate's) level at their institutions and funneled them to graduate or professional schools.

Proctor was dignified and intimidating. "I don't know if you are really ready for this. You are kind of up in age," he said. I think that statement was intended to challenge me or to see just how serious I was.

"Well, don't look at my age," I responded. He then said how demanding the program was.

"Tell me this. Has anyone finished the program?" I asked.

"Oh, yes! Several have even completed their doctorates. Several of my former students from Virginia have completed the program."

"Well," I told him, "if some others have finished it, then I can do it."

He perked up. "Well, I like that spirit, but it's not up to me to decide alone. There is a committee. You have to appear before them and they will make the final recommendations. This committee is made up of educators and civic leaders."

"Okay," I told him.

"I'll put your name on the list to be interviewed and they will contact you," he said.

Not long after, I met with the COP program committee. I can only remember two questions that they asked. The first was, "Tell us about yourself." I must have gone on for at least forty minutes telling them about my days in high school in Pensacola, and moving to New York in the 1930s. I also told them about the many bands I had played with, going back to Ray Shep. When I mentioned names like Lionel Hampton, Andy Kirk, Cab Calloway, Billie Holiday, Charlie Parker, Ivory Joe Hunter, and Louis Armstrong (who had died a few years before), I got approving nods from certain members of the committee. Some committee members looked at each other incredulously. It was then that I realized how *many* groups and well-known names I had actually been with.

I told them about my travels in Europe and starting Carnival Records. The second question I was asked was how many states I had traveled to. I paused for a minute and couldn't think of a single state in this country that I had not been to at least twice if not more. I was in the room for close to two hours.

After the interview, one woman, who seemed especially intrigued with what I had said, came out in the hall and stopped me as I was leaving. She said, "Mr. Evans, your talk was very interesting and you show a great deal of motivation. I promise you, if anybody is selected, you'll be one of them."

·　·　·　·　·

The fall semester of 1973, I entered the School of Education at Rutgers University along with twenty-four other students in the COP program. The class was a real rainbow coalition. There were poor whites, Native, Hispanic,

Asian, Italian, and African American people from around the country. Some of them had been out in life and had come back to school, but they were still all younger than me. Most of the participants were very smart, but I didn't sense any significant cut-throat competition among them.

I took courses like Philosophy of Education, Sociology of Education, History of Education, Statistics, Test and Measurement Instruments, and specialized seminars that required a lot of writing. In some classes, we had one paper each week. When I did have room for electives, I tended to take African American Studies courses. I took a few of these courses from Dr. Proctor, who was also my advisor. I came to be very close to him. I think because I was the oldest student in that COP class, he took particular interest in my development. He had told me it would be strenuous and he wasn't kidding, especially with that damn statistics course, and I was commuting back and forth between Newark and New Brunswick by train. I could have stayed down there if I wanted to be closer, but Anna and I were relatively settled in Newark.

I couldn't imagine life without Anna. My first wife, Taudry, and I didn't work as a couple. Perhaps it was all my traveling, but I don't think it would have lasted were I home every night. When it was over, it was over. I am grateful, though, that Anna came along. She was my partner and friend. The best part of our relationship was that she never let me get away with procrastinating. "Go, do not stay," she'd say.

Many men I know had their wives tell them what they couldn't or shouldn't do. With Anna it was, "Yes, you can," or "Yes, you will do it." If something went wrong, she was right there to catch me. She never let me be content with just growing old.

· · · · ·

I closed down the Branford Place office and moved my material back home, installed an answering machine to take messages dealing with Carnival Records, and arranged with Livingstone Audio Productions to re-release two Manhattans albums, *Dedicated to You* and *For You and Yours* on the eight-track format. I later signed similar leasing arrangements with other companies.

Yet, I could not resist taking on another group. One day, a boy named Harry Simpkins, whose nickname was "Suitcase," came to my house to talk to me about his singing group. I was somewhat reluctant, but he was both persistent and persuasive. Stalling him, I told him to bring me a tape of the group. Once I heard it, I had the entire group come to my house. The ensemble included Harry Simpkins, Eugene Cohen, Neil Page, and

Valerie Scott. They had a name, but I didn't like it so I changed it to the Pretenders. Valerie participated in the group's first recording, which was "I Call It Love," but then left the group because her husband didn't want her to tour. It was another one of those Barbara Brown scenarios; the only difference was that Valerie's husband had a singing career and had toured himself. She was replaced by Patricia Tandy, who fit right into the group like a glove and was even stronger than Valerie.

The Pretenders hit with "Just You Wait and See," "Hearts Were Made to Love," and "I'll Love You for the Rest of My Days," which was written by Kenny Ruffin. They also recorded new versions of several Manhattans hits, including "I'm the One That Love Forgot" and "I Wanna Be."

I used to book the Pretenders with groups like the Chi-Lites, Kool and the Gang, the Persuaders, the Intruders, the Main Ingredients, and the Drifters. Most of them were out of Philadelphia and Washington, where the Pretenders had a consistent following.

* * * * *

As the two-year program ended, I was approaching my sixtieth birthday. The other members of the class were preparing their resumés, but I figured I was too old to be doing that. Some of them persuaded me to prepare mine, so I did and sent it around with the rest of theirs. I finished the program at the end of 1974 and received my Master's in Education from Rutgers in January 1975. During the commencement ceremony that May, I noticed that my former counselor, Calvin Woodland, from Essex County College was receiving his Ph.D. at the same time. We smiled and nodded to each other to acknowledge that we had both come a long way.

* * * * *

For six months, I worked as an adjunct professor in the Department of Music at Essex County College. I taught saxophone, flute, clarinet, and a course entitled Black Contributions to Music. Occasionally, I was invited to lecture at the Paul Robeson Center at Rutgers in New Brunswick. Then I accepted a position using my research experience with the State of New Jersey. Muh would have been proud to see me with a college degree and a steady, good-paying job.

* * * * *

Investigating for the Department of Dairy Industry (DDI) was the state job I landed. Merchants and store owners liked my easy-going style because other investigators had apparently been heavy-handed with them in the past. I didn't have to report to an office. Assigned a state car, I simply left from home. On more than one occasion, my facility with Italian came in handy. After a few years I was promoted to a senior investigator. In that capacity, I had the authority to collect money for licenses and fines. When an establishment was outside the regulation, I could assess them a fine for the violations. When the severity of the situation called for it, I could issue a summons and have the offending establishment or individual appear at a hearing in Trenton.

Once in Harrison, New Jersey, I found myself on the receiving end of the law. Harrison is just across the Passaic River from Newark. I parked my car in front of a storefront, strolled in, and started asking my routine questions.

"Can I check your dairy license? Who are your suppliers? Where is your price list on the milk? What do you charge for a gallon, half gallon, a quart?"

The owner stalled an employee at the counter and headed for a back room. A few minutes later, four police cars pulled up outside as if to surround the store. The police jumped out and stood outside the door. Just as I opened my mouth to say, "Hey, something's going on out here," the police burst in and pointed their guns at me!

I could barely get the words out. I told the police who I was, and they asked for my identification. Unfortunately, I had left it in my suit from the day before. I pointed out to my state car, told them there was second identification there, and asked them to look at it, which they declined to do. I then asked them to call the DDI in Trenton to verify my employment and identity. As it turned out, my boss, a great guy named Joe Jones, was out of the office.

Joe Jones and I had a shaky relationship initially but eventually became the best of friends. In many ways, we transcended racial barriers. Our first encounter set that stage.

"Let me tell you something right up front. I'm a prejudiced son of a bitch," he said.

"Oh, that's nothing," I said looking him back in the eyes. "By the way, guess what? So am I."

We both laughed. Once that was cleared up, we were just fine. He called me "Doctor" because I had the degree from Rutgers. I really did educate him on a number of issues, including African American firsts, among other things.

Finally, the lead cop told me that I resembled a man who had swindled some people out of their money the week before. He showed me a picture of the swindler. He was much younger, with facial hair and a large Afro. I pulled off my cap to expose my balding head and said sarcastically, "I can see the resemblance. I wish I had the hair that son of a bitch has."

Joe Jones, in the meantime, found out about what had happened and threatened to have someone from the state's attorney's office intervene if they didn't release me. The cops let me go. I laughed it off, but I was angry inside. Joe also sent another investigator to that store that called the police on me, and the owners were fined three hundred dollars for multiple violations.

Racism is still alive and well in America. I've come to terms with it, but like most black men, I can't ever put it behind me. Fortunately, there are fair-minded whites, too, like Joe Jones.

• • • • •

By the early 1980s I was kind of coasting along enjoying what I was doing with the State of New Jersey. Occasionally, I would dabble in the music business to see what was happening. I'd check the trade journals, to see who was big, what kind of things they were recording, and following what the trends were.

Carnival Records was almost twenty years old. I hadn't released anything for several years, but that was to change shortly, thanks to Alto Lee. He owned two large stores, Lee's Records, in East Orange and in Newark. I would go in the East Orange store on occasion and Lee would keep me posted on what records were selling. One day, he asked me to listen to a tape of this group called the New Jersey Connection. He kept telling me how good they were and persuaded me to record them on the Carnival label. The New Jersey Connection released a forty-five, "Love Don't Come Easy," as a vocal version on side A and an instrumental version on side B of the record. It was moderately successful, but it opened up several opportunities for the group. They were offered a chance to tour England because their release had done well over there. They couldn't get things together because of internal politics and personality conflicts. This same problem caused them to miss another major opportunity in New York. It was an old familiar story of a group with one major hit only to fall by the wayside because they failed to seize upon the momentum. It was an all too common tune in the record business.

• • • • •

Around the same time, I got a phone message from a company out west. Joe Jones called me at home to tell me a man named Rico Tee had called the office and wanted to talk to me about some music. I reached Rico Tee in San Francisco, and he said, "Hey, Joe!" It was as if he had known me for years, but I swear I couldn't remember him.

"Man, I've been trying to find you for months! I was in New York a few months ago and nobody knew where you were." Somehow he found out I was with the New Jersey Department of Agriculture. Later, in a 1981 *Bill-board* article, Rico said he "tracked [me] down like Kojak."

Rico was well schooled in the record trade. He was working for Solid Smoke Records, a San Francisco–based label that specialized in rereleases. Solid Smoke wanted to reissue two Manhattans albums. Rico did all the negotiating over the phone, so I never actually saw him face to face. He was very professional and had the contract to me within a day of our conversation. The reissue did quite well, because by the early 1980s the Manhattans had become million-sellers on Columbia and a younger generation was being exposed to their earlier works.

Most of my European catalog leasing arrangements are handled by Ace Records in the United Kingdom. I'll have to back up a little to tell how that affiliation came about. When I started Carnival Records in the early 1960s, I would periodically receive letters from this kid in London, Trevor Churchill. He routinely requested Manhattans songs and those of the other Carnival artists. When I was approached by Ace Records in the early 1980s about a leasing arrangement, I noticed the name Trevor Churchill was listed as president of the company. Ace Records subsequently took over the entire Carnival catalog for their European markets.

· · · · ·

One day in the early 1980s, I received an interesting piece of mail:

> 1402 East Leonard Street
> Pensacola, Florida 32503
> September 6, 1983

Mr. Joe Evans
1238 Lansdown Terrace
Plainfield, New Jersey

Dear Mr. Evans:

The Music Makers Hall of Fame's Fourth Annual Celebration will be held in Pensacola, Florida, July 6, 7, and 8, 1984. A Jazz Workshop will be held on the 6th and 7th of July, and the Fourth Annual Hall of Fame Induction will be held on July 8, 1984. You have received a unanimous vote to be inducted into the 1984 Hall of Fame.

Please send at once, a 5x7 color photo of yourself, and a complete resumé. We would also like for you to perform during our two (2) day Jazz Workshop if possible.

We congratulate you on your nomination for induction into the Music Makers Hall of Fame.

Sincerely,
Tony R. McCray, Sr.
Chairman of the Board

Since I had left Pensacola in 1938, this relatively small southern town had produced its share of musicians, including the saxophonists Gigi Gryce and Junior Cook (both of whom had also studied with Ray Shep), the jazz pianists Ida Goodson and Joe Occhipint, and the drummer Eddie Williams, among many others. Of course, there was my childhood friend, Bobby Johnson, whose own career had flourished with Erskine Hawkins and Benny Carter, and who was still going strong at the time in the resort area of Ellenville in upstate New York. Bobby was inducted into the Hall of Fame the year before me.

When I arrived at the airport in Pensacola, a long white limousine and driver met me and virtually rolled out the red carpet. Once I arrived at the hotel, I got visits from Robert "Snookie" Willis and Johnny Warren, both of whom were in the Ray Shep band with me. Snookie told me that Shep had died just a few years earlier.

I had actually been back to Pensacola a few times over the years, but it was typically with a band and wasn't a long stay, so I didn't really follow how well the city had grown up. I told them that I was often teased about being from Pensacola. Musicians frequently referred to the town as "Pepsicola" and me as "Pepsicola Joe." There was a time when you could have blindfolded me and I couldn't have gotten lost in that city; however, by 1984, I hardly knew where I was.

The Hall of Fame induction ceremony was quite moving. The other inductees were a concert pianist, Donald Shirley; two jazz saxophonists, Herman Junior Cook and Thomas Gryce; and a retired university bandleader, Leander Kirsey. After each of us was presented with our award, we got the opportunity to speak about our careers. Although Pensacola wasn't home for me anymore, I was very honored by the welcome and the gesture of receiving the award.

· · · · ·

I have come to learn there are certain things that you can't control, and in those instances life can be a gamble. I took the hand I was dealt and played it. Throughout my career I made necessary choices to do mundane things like pay the rent. I was always reliable and was never late for a performance. My music was my livelihood and I tried to practice it as a businessman would. People like Charlie Parker didn't worry about such things. He just played with passion and abandon. He and many others I knew personally had far bigger recognition and rewards, but many of them also paid higher prices. I am convinced you can also develop genius through work, drill, and repetition. I have bobbed and weaved my way through enough situations and taken enough punches to know. Some of that wisdom comes with age.

But a lot of my success I owed to the musicians I worked with and experiences that influenced me throughout the years. My first real teacher, Shep, for example, is still part of my life. He carried himself with dignity. He was quiet and respectful. Those characteristics became a part of my personality. There were others like Benny Carter whom I also looked up to, respected as artists and as sophisticated men. I respected Charlie Parker's genius as a musician, but his "habit" was a warning to me about what drugs could do to you; no matter how talented you were, they could take you out. I saw too many cases where that happened. I didn't want no part of it. I always did feel sorry for Billie Holiday, though. She was such a kind lady.

I looked to Louis Armstrong as someone special. I thought of him as a historical figure even when I was with him. He *was* jazz. When I was a kid I heard him on the radio. He was way ahead of everybody. I felt I was lucky to be close to a man like that. I also learned from him that greatness didn't have to cause a person to lose their identity. In many ways, he was like every other band member, although the public regarded him as some kind of hero and he deserved it.

When I went to Lionel Hampton I absorbed other lessons because I was quite seasoned as a musician by then. The first thing I noticed about Hamp was how hard he worked. He didn't have to work so hard because he was so talented, but he did anyway. He went all out. He always wanted people to feel they were getting their money's worth. He was a great artist and I felt privileged to work with him. Cab Calloway was also a good showman like Hamp, but not a great musician. The thing that I liked about Cab was that he had great musicians working for him and that was his strength because we made him look good. His was what I would call an example of genius developed through hard work.

Johnny Hodges was also a dignified and respectable man. When I was young, he was my idol. He was the ideal saxophonist until I met Benny Carter, who could play several instruments, compose, and arrange. It seems there was nothing he couldn't do.

One influence who stands out as both a musician and a person was someone who, unfortunately, I never played with. That was Duke Ellington. Many black bandleaders of his and later eras thought they had to be showmen and went overboard with minstrel or clown-like behavior, with the wide grin and bulging eyes, with raised eyebrows, and the Stepin Fetchit gestures. In all the times I saw Duke perform he never behaved in that manner. Even when he appeared in movies, he never played a shoeshine boy or butler like many others felt compelled to. He was always suave and dignified. He maintained that image throughout his life. His music was fabulous. He was the ideal bandleader.

Lastly, I learned from my teacher and coauthor Christopher Brooks that there are people whom I can trust to help me tell my story. I took a black music course that he taught, and even though he is young enough to be my grandson, I learned things from him that I didn't know. I am confident that with people like him around, the era that I lived through and the people I came in contact with will live on.

Epilogue

Long Good-byes

This story was to have ended in the mid-1990s with my eightieth birthday. Although I never imagined I would make it this far, I turned ninety-one on October 7, 2007. But the last several years have been punctuated with a loneliness and sadness that I can barely describe. The most significant is that I lost my beloved Anna.

In the summer of 1998, Anna began having symptoms of fatigue, malaise, and general lack of energy. We both assumed that it had something to do with an earlier diagnosed condition she had, temporal arteritis. She broke out in shingles, which had chickenpox-like symptoms. There were several doctors' visits and blood tests, but they kept getting misinterpreted. After several attempts the correct diagnosis finally came—acute leukemia malagia, cancer of the blood. When I first heard the word leukemia, I thought *my* life was about to be over.

Her primary physician, Dr. May, mapped out several strategies and the likely scenarios that could result. We could do nothing and allow the disease to progress, or we could pursue a chemotherapy regimen. We were warned about the reality that at seventy-four years old and with a heart murmur (the result of a childhood case of rheumatic fever) Anna might not have a strong outcome. We discussed these options with family members and close friends and decided to pursue the chemotherapy route. I read studies about cancer of the blood being reversed in places like Brazil and even considered taking Anna there for treatment.

She was admitted to the hospital at the end of October. I mostly stayed there with her. She was a real trouper throughout. Anna charmed the hospital staff with her manners and pleasant nature, although they (and I) knew the gravity of what she was about to undergo. We saw an herbalist who spoke in promising terms but made clear he was not a medical practitioner and did not guarantee anything. His interest was in lessening the toxic effects of the chemotherapy.

Gradually Anna began losing her appetite, a normal reaction to the regimen. When I wasn't at the hospital, Louise came from New Jersey religiously and Christopher Brooks was also standing in to help out there. Several friends came through to visit. She had made so many of them over the years, there was little wonder. After Thanksgiving, the chemo regimen was over, and she came home. It had been a rough several weeks.

There was a bright spot in all this. On December 6, 1998, Anna celebrated her seventy-fifth birthday. Brooks hosted a party for her of more than forty friends and well-wishers. Her strength was marginal, but she was right there dressed in a beautiful pink suit. Everyone commented on how well she looked. The cancer went into remission, but we had to continue our doctor's visits to check on her platelet levels. As a result of the chemo they had increased.

I attended seminars, visited agencies, and sat in on support groups about living with people with cancer. I even attended a one-woman show (by a cancer survivor) in which the actress was joking about the disease, which she referred to as "the big C." I was not willing to look at any possibility other than Anna's complete recovery. The alternative was unimaginable. Her appetite began to decrease again, which caused her to lose weight noticeably. Given that her immune system was low, we had to take certain precautions with visitors who might compromise it. That meant people with colds or sneezes had to stay away or wear masks and gloves while in her presence. Louise still made the six-hour drive from New Jersey to help out, and I suspended my usual walking schedule to take care of Anna. I was afraid to get sick. Anna had always taken care of me in the past; it was now time for me to stand up and be counted.

In my heart I knew she was dying, but I couldn't say anything to her that suggested it. I was so convincing that I believe she thought I was in denial. I had already known from a friend who had not survived a month after getting a leukemia diagnosis that it was usually fatal.

The primary physician made us aware of an experimental study being simultaneously run at the Medical College of Virginia and A. D. Anderson Cancer Clinic in Houston. We consulted with the physician leading the study, who thought Anna would be a good candidate for it. The last part of June 1999 she was admitted to the program. She was to stay in the hospital for four weeks. As usual, she was the darling of the hospital staff. She rarely complained to the nursing staff even when she was in discomfort. She was again released at the end of July and received a visit from her friend of over fifty years, Dr. Carrie Saunders. We even took a few short outings. Anna had noticeably lost weight, but since I saw her on a regular basis, I didn't notice as much. She continued to handle all the bills and insisted on doing all the paper work regarding her hospital stays and treatments.

We celebrated my eighty-third birthday on Saturday, October 9, 1999 (which was two days after the actual date). I remember the event so well because Anna was real upbeat. She had a healthy appetite for the small gathering that Brooks had arranged at our house. She gave me a birthday card that read in part, "I am thinking of you and feeling feelings of love." It was the last time my wife was herself.

The following day she woke up and was not feeling well. I offered to stay home from church, but she insisted that I go. When I got back she was becoming more disoriented and was unable to respond to basic questions like remembering her sisters' names. We decided that she needed to go to the hospital. The ambulance attendants arrived and, as usual, she was a perfect lady. The effects of the chemotherapy regimen had taken its toll on her system.

By the following Tuesday Anna was in and out of consciousness. When she was conscious, she complained about being too hot and kept kicking the sheets off of her. I fanned her and at some point she seemed to fall asleep. Louise and I stayed at her bedside. About 4:30 A.M. Wednesday, Louise said, "Joe, Annie has stopped breathing." I called a nurse, who confirmed that she had slipped quietly away. I was only slightly comforted when I thought to myself that the last touch she felt was mine. I was actually holding her hand at the time but didn't realize she had gone. She had signed a Do Not Resuscitate order so there was no possibility of reviving her. I know she was tired of the entire ordeal. I think she had held on as long as she did in part for me. I had suffered the deaths of many family members, including Muh, Roy Lee, and Daddy, but this was the worst experience with death I had ever known.

Unbeknownst to me, Annie had spoken to Brooks about doing her funeral arrangements because she knew I would have difficulty laying her to rest. The process, however, was relatively smooth. Although she was a Jehovah's Witness, the other family members felt their funerary practices were too low-key by their standards (i.e., without emotional preaching and singing) and opted to have the service at the funeral home. Consistent with Witness practice, those members and friends from her religious community had to leave once the service began because, by custom, they are not allowed to attend other faiths' religious services.

The funeral was emotional. I thought seeing her in that casket would cause my heart to break. The reality that it was the last time I would see her caused me to break down repeatedly. Her brother, Charlie, had come from Florida, and her older sister, Gertrude, was also there from New Jersey. Although Anna was not the oldest sister in the family, she managed most of the family affairs and she typically had the strongest voice in such matters. Her death was a loss for them as well. It was the saddest event of my life.

By the end of 1999, Anna's sister Gertrude had also passed away, and my granddaughter, Jeanie, had died of lupus. She left behind a child, my only great-grandson, Milton Evans, who should be about ten now. I get to see this little feisty boy every couple of months.

I also lost my lifetime friend Bobby Johnson in June 2001. He was still playing trumpet into his eighties. He was living in upstate New York and playing twice a week with a band in the area. Toye and I went to see him in the hospital the week he died. He was not entirely lucid when we saw him. I was not entirely convinced he knew it was me. The following year, Taudry died in Florida. I had not seen her for the better part of forty-five years. My son, Tommy, went to the funeral and told me about it afterwards. I have outlived both the women I was married to, but both were important to me in their respective ways.

At over ninety years old I have lived to see a new century as well as a new social order. There was a time when I would have gone cold at seeing white and black people socializing as they do now in Richmond, Virginia. We all knew blacks and whites sneaked around behind closed doors and at night. The results would often be, for example, like the case of the daughter of Strom Thurmond, the late South Carolina senator. But when you can see a black person walk up and kiss a white person on the lips in the street, it is definitely a different South than the one I grew up in. When I hear people say things haven't changed in this country with regard to race, I think to myself, "Oh, yes, they have." In these days of political correctness, when a public figure or celebrity can lose their job for an off-the-cuff remark or slip-of-the-tongue racial slur about African Americans, Jews, or Hispanics, things *have* changed.

Sometimes I think about producing a new song or helping a local act get going in the business, but so far I have contented myself with the occasional contact from some television or movie producer wanting to use one of the songs from the Carnival catalog. I am sometimes amazed at how they find me, but they always manage.

I don't know how much time I have left, but I do believe Christopher Brooks and I have given a good representation of my life here. Sometimes I feel I have lived more than one life. There aren't many people who have had the opportunity to perform with as many celebrated personalities as I have, start their own business, and also live to see many new generations of musicians carry forward a musical tradition that seems destined to continue.

• • • • •

There is a song that summarizes how I sometimes feel at this point in my life: "I'll Be Seeing You," written by Irving Kahal and Sammy Fain. As far as I am concerned, nobody delivered it quite like Billie Holiday. No matter how many times she sang that song when I was performing with her, I never failed to be moved. That line "In all the familiar places" is like a person trying hard not to say good-bye or let go of someone very dear to them. So even when the absent person is not physically present (as in death), the performer will be reminded of the impact they had on them and their life. Well, there are many people who had that impact on me. I believe I will see them all again.

When Billie delivered the line "I'll find you in the morning sun, and when the night is new," there was no doubt that she was singing about her life experience. The final line, however, was her coup de grace. It regularly left many people, including several of us in the band, in tears:

> I'll be looking at the moon
> But I'll be seeing you.

That's all for now.

Discography

Carnival Records, 605 West 156th Street, New York, N.Y.
Songs arranged and produced by Joe Evans (abridged list)

RECORD NUMBER	ARTIST	SONG	MASTER NUMBER
501	The Tren-Teens	"Your Yah-Yah Is Gone"	1001A
		"My Baby's Gone"	1001B
502	Delores Johnson	"What Kind of Man Are You?"	1002A
		"Try Me One More Time"	1002B
503	Barbara Brown	"Send Him to Me"	1003
		"Sometimes I Wonder"	1004
504	The Manhattans	"I've Got Everything but You"	1005
		"Call Somebody Please"	1010
507	The Manhattans	"I Wanna Be (Your Everything)"	1011
		"What's It Gonna Be"	1012

RECORD NUMBER	ARTIST	SONG	MASTER NUMBER
508	Barbara Brown	"So in Love"	1013
		"Forget Him"	1014
512	The Manhattans	"The Boston Monkey"	1021
		"Follow Your Heart"*	1022
513	Phil Terrell	"I'll Erase You (From My Heart)"	1023
		"I'm Just a Young Boy"	1024
516	Harry Caldwell	"Please Come Back"	1029
		"Nobody Loves Me (Like My Baby)"	1030
517	The Manhattans	"Can I"*	1031
		"That New Girl"	1032
518	The Lovettes	"Little Miss Soul"	1033
		"Lonely Girl"	1034
521	Lee Williams and the Cymbals	"I Love You More"	1039
		"I'll Be Gone"	1040
522	The Manhattans	"I Bet'cha (Couldn't Love Me)"	1041
		"Sweet Little Girl"	1042
523	Phil Terrell	"Don't You Run Away"	1043
		"Love Has Passed Me By"	1044
526	The Manhattans	"All I Need Is Your Love"	1049
		"Our Love Will Never Die"	1050
527	Lee Williams and the Cymbals	"Peepin' (Through the Window)"	1051
		"Lost Love"	1052
530	The Lovettes	"I Need a Guy"	1057
		"I'm Afraid (To Say I Love You)"	1058
532	Lee Williams and the Cymbals	"Please Say It Isn't So"*	1061
		"Shing-a-Ling U.S.A."	1062
533	The Manhattans	"I Call It Love"	1063
		"Manhattan Stomp"	1064
535	The Turner Brothers	"I'm the Man for You, Baby"	1067
		"My Love Is Yours Tonight"	1068
536	Kenneth Ruffin	"I'll Keep Holding On"	1069
		"Cry, Cry, Cry"	1070
540	Lee Williams and the Cymbals	"'Til You Come Back to Me"*	1076
		"Love Is Breaking Out (All Over)"	1077

RECORD NUMBER	ARTIST	SONG	MASTER NUMBER
545	The Manhattans	"Call Somebody Please"	1010
		"'Til You Come Back to Me"*	1084
546	The Symphonies	"Need Someone to Love"	1083
		"That's What Love Will Do"	1085
547	Harry Caldwell	"Nobody Loves Me (Like My Baby)"	1030
		"A New World Is Just Beginning"*	1086
551	The Three Reasons	"Go Right On"	1092
		"Go Right On" (instru.)	1093
552	The Pretenders	"I Wanna Be (Your Everything)"	1087
		"Hearts Were Made to Love"*	1094
557	The Pretenders	"What Is Love"*	1097
		"I'm the One That Love Forgot"	1100
580	The New Jersey Connection	"Love Don't Come Easy"	1200
		"Love Don't Come Easy" (instru.)	1201

* Indicates songs written or cowritten by Joe Evans

Index

· · · · ·

JOE EVANS is an alto saxophonist, composer, and arranger who between 1939 and the mid-1960s performed with some of America's greatest musicians, including Louis Armstrong, Charlie Parker, and Lionel Hampton. As an entrepreneur, Evans worked with Cee Jay Records and founded Carnival Records.

· · · · ·

CHRISTOPHER BROOKS is a professor of anthropology in the School of World Studies at Virginia Commonwealth University in Richmond, Virginia. He holds a joint appointment in the Department of African American Studies. A seasoned biographer, he has produced several book-length studies, including *I Never Walked Alone: The Autobiography of an American Singer.* He has written numerous articles that have appeared in scholarly journals such as *American Anthropologist, International Review of African American Art, Literary Griot, Black Sacred Music, International Journal of Black Oral and Literary Studies,* and *African American Review.* He is a contributor to *The Greenwood Encyclopedia of African American Folklore.* As a Senior Fulbright Researcher in 1999–2000, Brooks examined women's rights organizations and their response to the HIV/AIDS pandemic in Zimbabwe and South Africa. He was also a Senior Research Fellow at the Southern African Research Institute for Policy Studies (SARIPS) in Harare, Zimbabwe (now called SAPES Trust).

· · · · ·

African American Music
in Global Perspective

Black Women and Music: More than the Blues
Edited by Eileen M. Hayes and Linda F. Williams

Ramblin' on My Mind: New Perspectives on the Blues
Edited by David Evans

Follow Your Heart: Moving with the Giants
of Jazz, Swing, and Rhythm and Blues
Joe Evans with Christopher Brooks

The University of Illinois Press
is a founding member of the
Association of American University Presses.

Composed in 9.5/13 Stone Serif
with Futura display
by Celia Shapland
at the University of Illinois Press
Designed by Copenhaver Cumpston
Manufactured by Sheridan Books, Inc.

UNIVERSITY OF ILLINOIS PRESS
1325 South Oak Street   Champaign, IL 61820-6903
www.press.uillinois.edu